D0211790

Praise for *While My Sol...*

"*While My Soldier* Serves is a book for anyon[e] ...ing in the military. Written by a mother who ......... war, the prayers in this book are not drawn from a denomination's book of prayers but lifted from the pages of the heart. This book isn't read—it is experienced."

Alton Gansky, novelist and author of *30 Events That Shaped the Church*

"As someone whose brother is in the military, I've been waiting for a book like this. Edie offers heartfelt advice and insights to help you pray your loved ones back home."

Steven James, national best-selling author of *Checkmate*

"*While My Soldier Serves* is an invaluable tool for those experiencing the distance and heartache of a loved one deployed. This book is a gem for those facing a situation that may leave them feeling powerless and afraid for what their loved one may be facing in the war theater. With these prayers, Melson not only holds the hands of military families, she kneels with them seeking guidance, wisdom, and counsel!"

Ronie Kendig, best-selling, award-winning author of
the *Quiet Professionals*

"No one knows what it means to pray for a loved one in the military like someone who has lived through it. While your loved one serves to protect America's freedom, Edie Melson will guide you with prayer, offering comfort through Scripture and a reminder that God is as close to you as He is to your soldier."

Eva Marie Everson, best-selling author of *Five Brides*

"The reality of death and destruction isn't mere concept to men and women in the military. It's a fact of life. For parents, spouses, family, and friends left behind, that reality can be paralyzing. As the mother of a former Marine, Edie Melson knows that feeling first-hand. In her newest book, *While My Soldier Serves: Prayers for Those with Loved Ones in the Military*, Edie shares real-life prayers, written from her heart, directed to the Creator and Protector of all."

Vonda Skelton, author of *Seeing Through the Lies*,
speaker, and wife of disabled veteran

"Author Edie Melson lives her passion for supporting military families. *While My Soldier Serves* exemplifies her dedication—and her ability to use her personal experience to embrace others who are struggling with fear and anxiety and seeking to support loved ones who are in harm's way. The book also provides powerful insight for those of us who do not have family in active service. Reading it brought me into the world of the prayerful parent, wife, sibling, or child and gave me the opportunity to reflect on the debt we owe those who serve our country both abroad and at home. *While My Soldier Serves* is an invitation to empathy and a glimpse into the power of faith."

Anne Kelly Tromsness, education director, The Warehouse Theatre
(South Carolina's only Blue Star Theatre)

"In light of recent blockbuster movies that give us a look into the lives of military families and the dark hole they enter, Edie Melson addresses those needs in this book of prayers designed to strengthen those at home who hold the ropes for these brave soldiers. As one who has been there, she offers honesty, hope, and comfort as she nourishes you in God's Word and carries you into His presence through the power of prayer."

Ginny Dent Brant, author of *Finding True Freedom:*
*From the White House to the World*

"God hears our prayers, but His heart pours out to the prayers of a loving mother. Especially when her prayers are pleas for the safety of her child. Melson has put pen to her own heartfelt and sometimes desperate cries in prayer to the God of all creation. These prayers will warm your soul, offer you guidance as you pray, and focus your heart to the feet of Jesus. A touching book of sweet words over the men and women who defend our country."

Cindy Sproles, author of *Mercy's Rain* and *New Sheets*

"Drawing from her experience as a military mom, Edie Melson equips you to be your loved one's 'spiritual ground support.' She pens the words that help you pray instead of worry. Within the pages of *While My Soldier Serves* you will find the words to help you turn anxiety into powerful intercession."

Beth K. Vogt, wife of a former Air Force officer who served for 24 years,
and author of *Somebody Like You* (selected by *Publisher's Weekly*
as one of its Best Books of 2014)

"About Christ, the Bible says there is no greater love than Christ's willingness to 'lay down his life for his friends.' Likewise, our brave men and women in the military are willing to show that Christ-like love on our behalf if it comes to that. The least we can do to repay that eternal debt is to lift them and their loved ones in prayer."

Steve Deace, nationally syndicated radio host

"Edie brings the service of a warrior and the sacrifice of the military family home to readers. This book will open your eyes to what the great men and women go through who keep our nation free. This book is also a reminder that Jesus is our High General who has everything well under control, even during times of war."

Major Jeff Struecker, retired, Black Hawk Down veteran

*While My Soldier Serves* draws the reader into the courts of God's presence with honesty and tenderness. All those who pray for the love and protection of a soldier or one serving actively in law enforcement will find the heartfelt supplications to God providing peace to the soul."

DiAnn Mills, award-winning author

"Edie Melson has put her finger (and her heart) on something desperately needed, especially today. We live in a world that is in turmoil and war is all around us. We all know at least one person affected by war. *While My Soldier Serves* is an incredible book that will encourage, inspire, and comfort those who have a loved one serving in the military. It also will serve as a reminder for those who don't, that the greatest gift we can give right now may be the gift of prayer."

Jack Eason, executive director, Crossover Ministries International

"This book is a must have for those who want to pray deeply and specifically for a deployed loved one. I wish I had this book when my husband was deployed. I look forward to recommending this book as a valuable resource to the military community."

Ginger Harrington, ministry leader for Planting Roots:
Strength to Thrive in Military Life

# WHILE
# MY SOLDIER
# SERVES

Copyright © 2015 by Edie Melson

Published by Worthy Inspired, an imprint of Worthy Publishing Group, a division of Worthy Media, Inc. 134 Franklin Road, Suite 200, Brentwood, Tennessee 37027.

WORTHY is a registered trademark of Worthy Media, Inc.

HELPING PEOPLE EXPERIENCE THE HEART OF GOD

---

Library of Congress Cataloging-in-Publication Data

Melson, Edie.
  While my soldier serves : prayers for those with loved ones in the military / Edie Melson.
    pages cm
  Includes bibliographical references and index.
  ISBN 978-1-61795-589-1 (hardcover : alk. paper)
  1. Armed Forces--Prayers and devotions.  I. Title.
  BV273.M45 2015
  242'.88--dc23

                              2015008828

---

All rights reserved. No part of this publication may be reproduced, stored in a retrieval system, or transmitted in any form or by any means—electronic, mechanical, photocopy, recording, scanning, or other—except for brief quotations in critical reviews or articles, without the prior written permission of the publisher.

Scripture references marked NKJV are from the Holy Bible, New King James Version. Copyright © 1982 by Thomas Nelson, Inc. Used by permission. | Scripture references marked NCV are from the New Century Version®. Copyright © 1987, 1988, 1991 by Word Publishing, a division of Thomas Nelson, Inc. All rights reserved. Used by permission. | Scripture references marked HCSB are from the Holman Christian Standard Bible™ Copyright © 2009, 2003, 2002, 2000, 1999 by Holman Bible Publishers. Used by permission. All rights reserved. | Scripture references marked NIV are from the Holy Bible, New International Version®. Copyright © 1973, 1978, 1984, 2011 International Bible Society. Used by permission of Zondervan. All rights reserved. | Scripture references marked NASB are from the New American Standard Bible®. Copyright © 1960, 1962, 1963, 1968, 1971, 1972, 1973, 1975, 1977, 1995 by The Lockman Foundation. Used by permission. | Scripture references marked NIRV are from the New International Reader's Version, Copyright © 1995, 1996, 1998, 2014 by Biblica, Inc.®. Used by permission. All rights reserved worldwide.

ISBN 978-1-61795-589-1

Cover Design by Kim Russell / Wahoo Designs
Page Layout by Bart Dawson

Printed in the United States of America

1 2 3 4 5—LBM—19 18 17 16 15

# WHILE MY SOLDIER SERVES

---

*Prayers for Those with*
*Loved Ones in the Military*

---

## EDIE MELSON

WORTHY
*Inspired*

This book is dedicated to two special people:

Our precious daughter-in-law,
Katie Melson,

Who walked through our son's deployments,
Supporting her husband, and us,
With beauty and grace.

★　★　★

And also to my husband,
Kirk Melson,

He's always seen the vision
Of what God wants for me as a writer
Much clearer than me.

# TABLE OF CONTENTS

# ACKNOWLEDGMENTS

★ ★ ★

No book can ever see the light of day without an entire team of people moving it forward. That's especially true of this book!

First I want to thank those in my life who have given this project, and all of us involved, much needed prayer support. I'd especially like to mention Sheri and Brian Owens, Randy Harling, Steve Genoble (and the youth ministry at SFBC), Ashley Moore, Valorie Moore, Gloria Moore, Sarah Moore, Noelle Lawson, Mary Denman, Pam Zollman, Caroline Eschenberg, Alycia Morales, and especially my long-time writing partner, Vonda Skelton.

A special shout-out goes to my amazing (and in my opinion best) agent in the world, David Van Diest. I also want to express my heartfelt gratitude to Pamela Clements and the team at Worthy Publishing. You took my vision and made it shine.

Additionally, no writer is ever able to move ahead without other writers to share the journey. Thank you to all those who helped with proofing, including Cathy Baker, Marcia Moston, Deb Koontz Roberson, Tammie Fickas. I'm grateful to all my fellow writers who encourage me, especially Alton Gansky, Charity Tinnin, Erynn Newman, Jess Koschnitzky, Amanda Stevens, Beth Vogt, Susan May Warren, Alena Tauriainen, Melissa Tagg, Lisa Jordan, Michelle Lim, Rachel Hauck, and the gang from the Light Brigade.

Most of all I want to thank my amazing boys (and now girls, too), Jimmy and Katie Melson, Kirk and Weslyn Melson, and John Melson. They've always encouraged me and been my staunchest supporters.

# FOREWORD
## By Todd Starnes

★ ★ ★

Edie Melson is a Great American. She is a true patriot, a devoted wife, a loving mother. And she is my friend.

She is also a friend to the United States Armed Forces—the greatest fighting force on the planet. And that's why I am so honored to pen this foreword.

*While My Soldier Serves* should be in the homes of every military family in the nation. It's a collection of prayers and Bible verses and inspirational messages to not only encourage our brave fighting men and women but also the families left behind.

Edie reminds us that she has been where many military moms have been. Her oldest son served in the Marine Corps. He went straight from high school to boot camp to Iraq. She knows what it's like to stay up all night—filled with fear of the unknown—waiting for that phone call, that knock on the front door.

Having someone you love serving in the Armed Forces is a source of great pride and joy. But it's also a source of great uncertainty, knowing that your loved one might be in harm's way. And for those left behind, it can also be a time of great loneliness.

But these pages are filled with words of encouragement and purpose—prayers for both your soldier and yourself.

*While My Soldier Serves* is homespun and heartfelt. And you will get a glimpse of Edie's Southern roots tucked away in the pages of this delightful tome. (How else can you explain quotes from Mother Teresa and Eudora Welty—in the same book!)

While I was reading this book, I was reminded of a poignant moment in the film *We Were Soldiers*. Just before Mel Gibson's character was about to ship off to Vietnam, he took a moment to pray with his young daughter. The image of that barefoot girl and her father in combat boots kneeling side-by-side tugged at my heart strings.

*While My Soldier Serves* brings that Hollywood moment to real life. Edie reminds us that while our soldiers wage war on the front lines, our families wage a spiritual war on the home front. And this book will equip you to win that battle!

Thank you, Edie, for writing a book such as this for such a time as this. I hope these pages will bring you encouragement and assurance while your soldier serves.

Todd Starnes is a Fox News Channel
personality and author.

# INTRODUCTION

★  ★  ★

Many of us live daily with the reality that war is a part of life. We've sent someone we love off to war, and now we're left with our own battles to fight. Our adversaries include loneliness, fear, worry, and nightmares we can't share with those who haven't been in the trenches with us.

I've been where you are. Our oldest son went straight from high school graduation to Marine Corps Boot Camp to Iraq as a frontline infantry Marine. I know just how frightening it is to have a loved one in a life-and-death situation and be unable to do a single thing to help. I've sat up nights, filled with fear, trying to pray when words just wouldn't come.

Thousands of families send loved ones off to fight on a daily basis. These families spend a lot of time living in a world out of control. This kind of stress can take an incredible toll, but there is hope. When we feel helpless, we can take our fears to the One who loves us more than anything and holds the universe in His hands.

In this book you'll find the words to usher you into His presence. These prayers are a place to visit again and again as you take your own fears to God. They're just a starting point, written to help you find your own voice as you call out on behalf of the one you love.

Blessings,
Edie Melson

1

# HOW TO USE THIS BOOK

★　★　★

This book is written to be used by many people, in many situations—from the spouse or parents of a soldier, to the close friend, to everyone in between. In addition, because we have so many women serving in our armed services, the pronouns change from prayer to prayer. The best way to use this book is to insert your soldier's name in place of the pronouns.

This is also a good resource to use in a small group setting, as several come together to pray for those serving in our military and their families.

There are two main sections within this book: Prayers for My Soldier and Prayers for Me. While my son was deployed I discovered that when I took time to pray for myself, my prayers for my son came easier.

Within the two sections, the prayers are further organized into topics, with a more specific focus reflected in the titles of the individual prayers. You may choose to read the book straight through from beginning to end, or search for individual prayers that focus on the needs you and your soldier are currently facing.

The power of our prayers is amplified by the fact that so many of us are praying the same thing, at almost the same time, for those in our armed services. We can take encouragement from being a part of a great choir of voices, praying for our soldiers. When we each give voice to these prayers, we become a mighty concert, directed by the power of the amazing God we serve.

# PRAYERS FOR
# MY SOLDIER

# WISDOM

We all pray for our loved ones to be wise in the decisions they make. That's never more true than when the decisions could have life-and-death consequences.

# HELP MY SOLDIER MAKE WISE DECISIONS

★ ★ ★

"Be faithful in small things because it is
in them that your strength lies."

*Mother Teresa*

*Dear Lord,* I'm asking You to protect my loved one by helping him make wise decisions. I know at times he has to make split-second decisions—life-and-death decisions. Please give him the information he needs to choose wisely. I know he's exhausted and tired of the situation he's in. Don't let him make decisions that will harm him or those around him.

I also know he's far from home, and there are many temptations surrounding him. I ask that You give him the strength to resist the things that would harm him. Show him clearly the consequences of poor choices. Make his path clear, and put people around him to make choosing wisely easier.

Surround him with buddies who will support his good choices and point out his poor ones. Give him the friends he needs for this specific situation. No one knows what can happen when we choose one thing over another, but You do know. Let him hear You clearly as he decides what actions to take. Most of all protect him, even when he chooses poorly. Keep him in Your perfect care. Amen

★ ★ ★

*I declare the end from the beginning, and from long ago what is not yet done, saying: My plan will take place, and I will do all My will.*

*Isaiah 46:10 HCSB*

# GIVE MY LOVED ONE YOUR EYES TO SEE THE PLANS OF THE ENEMY

★ ★ ★

"Never think you've seen the last of anything."

*Eudora Welty*

*Dear Lord,* protect my loved one. I know the enemy she's facing is cruel and willing to do things we'd never consider. I know the Bible promises us that You are everywhere and see everything. Please keep watch over my loved one.

Give her the wisdom she needs to anticipate the traps of the enemy. Don't let them catch her unaware. Make sure she's alert when she needs to be. Keep her equipment in top condition and don't let her be stranded somewhere dangerous with no means of defense.

Be the first line of defense for my soldier by giving her insight into the ways the enemy wages war. Let the plans of her enemies be so transparent that they're obvious at all times.

Confuse her enemies and make them turn on one another instead of my soldier and those she's serving with. Attack her enemies with waves of discouragement and distrust of their own commanders until they lay down their weapons and surrender.

Most of all, guard my loved one when she sleeps. Keep her safe when she's too tired to focus. Show her what it means to trust in You at all times and in all ways. Amen

★ ★ ★

*So he answered, "Do not fear, for those who are with us are more than those who are with them."*

*2 Kings 6:16 NASB*

# GIVE MY SOLDIER A CLEAR HEAD

★ ★ ★

*"One who gains strength by overcoming obstacles possesses*
*the only strength which can overcome adversity."*
*Albert Schweitzer*

*Dear Lord,* my soldier is living in a dark place right now. He's surrounded by enemies. He's being stretched past the point of endurance physically and mentally. Yet, I know he has to keep a clear head so he will know the right thing to do. How is that even possible?

Give him the strength he needs to make good decisions. Protect him from confusion and distraction while he's out on patrol. His enemies could come at him any time, even masquerading as friends. Let him see into the heart of any person who approaches him, and make him able to judge correctly the intent of those who may wish him harm.

As he moves through enemy land, give him the foresight he needs to anticipate the obstacles that lie in his path. Show him where that wisdom comes from.

Set Your angels to guard his path. Do not let the enemy approach without warning. Surround my loved one with others who have Your insight and wisdom. Let them become stronger together than they could ever be were separately. Give him friends who share his clear mindedness. Guard him and all his comrades from harm. Amen

★ ★ ★

*If any of you lacks wisdom, you should ask God, who gives generously to*
*all without finding fault, and it will be given to you.*

*James 1:5 NIV*

# HELP MY LOVED ONE CHOOSE JOY

★  ★  ★

"Joy does not simply happen to us.
We have to choose joy and keep choosing it every day."

*Henri J. M. Nouwen*

*Dear Lord,* today let my loved one choose joy. Open her eyes to the good things that are taking place around her. I know she's surrounded by painful things. Everything is strange and uncomfortable, but give her reasons to laugh.

Let joy bubble up from deep inside, and make it contagious to those around her. I know no one rejoices in war, but I also know that You can bring beauty to light wherever she is.

Give her a taste, or a smell, or a sound that brings back happy memories. Then let those memories be translated into her life right now. The Bible promises that You are with us, no matter what. Let her find that to be so true that she will never doubt that again as long as she lives.

Provide my loved one with friends to share the joy and a safe place to rest in it. I know You can do this, in ways I can't even imagine, and I'm asking this for her. Give her a chance to get away from the ugliness that surrounds her, and continue to do this for her until she comes back home safe. Amen

★  ★  ★

*You, Lord, keep my lamp burning; my God turns my darkness into light.*

*Psalm 18:28 NIV*

# THANK YOU FOR YOUR STEADFAST LOVE

★ ★ ★

"Here's the paradox. We can fully embrace God's love only when we recognize how completely unworthy of it we are."

*Ann Tatlock*

*Dear Lord,* I love You so much. And as much as I love You, I know You love me even more. You would pay any price to make sure I'm safe. Within the confidence of that truth, I also know that You love my soldier.

There's nowhere too dangerous, nowhere too remote, nowhere too dark to separate us from Your love. Everywhere I look I see the evidence of Your great love. You show it in the friends who surround me, coming to help before I ask. You prove it in the home and family You've provided for me.

All of this is true for my soldier as well. You've put people around him to be there when he needs them. They encourage him, support him, and protect him. You don't love us in a vacuum. You love us in the context of a real and active community. Creation itself is a reflection of Your great love. Amen

★ ★ ★

*For I am persuaded that not even death or life, angels or rulers, things present or things to come, hostile powers, height or depth, or any other created thing will have the power to separate us from the love of God that is in Christ Jesus our Lord!*

*Romans 8:38-39 HCSB*

# MAY MY LOVED ONE SEE BEAUTY

★ ★ ★

"The very nature of joy makes nonsense of our common
distinction between having and wanting."

*C. S. Lewis*

*Dear Lord,* as I sit here my mind is drawn to all the things my
loved one must be experiencing. She's seeing so much right now,
horrible things that come with war. I also pray that she's seeing
some beautiful things in the midst of the ugliness. It's those things
I'm asking You for on her behalf today. Please surround her with
moments of beauty. Give her times of refreshing, glimpses of joy
and laughter. Help her save those memories for times when she sees
nothing but suffering.

I know she must be seeing some of the worst in people. I'm
asking You to balance that with moments of kindness and love.
Remind her that although this world can be an ugly place, You are
still at work and bringing good things to bear.

Let my loved one be an example of what's good. Work through
her to comfort others. Use her skills to protect those who need
protection. Then show her how vital she is to Your plan. Give her
examples of Your great love in her life and in the lives of those she
meets every day. Most of all, never let her give in to despair, but
always turn to You for comfort and peace. Amen

★ ★ ★

*Splendor and majesty are before Him, strength and beauty are in His
sanctuary.*

*Psalm 96:6 NASB*

# GIVE MY SOLDIER THE TOOLS TO DEAL WITH THE FEAR HE'S FACING

★ ★ ★

"Fear always springs from ignorance."

*Ralph Waldo Emerson*

*Dear Lord,* I can't imagine the fear that my soldier has to deal with right now. I know there are stretches of time when he'll be okay, but then those times hit when he's overwhelmed and terror threatens to overwhelm him. When those waves of fear wash over him, be there to catch him. Hold him close and let him know You're there.

Use the people around him as reassurance that You're still active in his life. Give him friends to share his struggles. Allow him glimpses of things that can only be from You so his faith will remain strong when the fear rolls in.

Give him the strength and stamina I know he needs. Beyond that, let him see the humor in the situations where he finds himself and experience the power behind shared laughter.

None of these things are easy, but I know You're a big God. Remind him that You're never too big to be involved in the life of one man. Show him how precious he is to You. Replace his fear with a sense of peace as You wrap him in Your love. Amen

★ ★ ★

*God has made us what we are. In Christ Jesus, God made us to do good works, which God planned in advance for us to live our lives doing.*

*Ephesians 2:10 NCV*

# HELP MY SOLDIER REMEMBER WHY SHE'S SERVING

★　★　★

"Our victory rests not on faith in our spirituality.
Our victory rests on faith in our God."

*Beth Moore*

*Dear Lord,* during this deployment help my soldier remember why she's there. I know the local people don't always appreciate her sacrifice, but give her reminders that at home we always do. She has such a tender heart and a spirit that wants to serve others. Make sure she has the opportunities to exercise those gifts.

She joined the military because of her willingness to sacrifice. Don't let her become bitter as she serves. Give her opportunities to see how her service is benefitting the country she's in as well as our country.

Show her that her sacrifice has meaning, not just here and now but for eternity. Provide her with the proof of Your pleasure in her willingness to follow Your plan for her life.

Remind my loved one that You always honor those who are willing to serve. Show her how much You love her heart of sacrifice. Don't let her fall into the trap of basing her self-worth on the attitudes of others toward her. Make sure she's looking to You and You only for the measure of her worth. Amen

★　★　★

*Do nothing out of selfish ambition or vain conceit. Rather, in humility value others above yourselves.*

*Philippians 2:3 NIV*

# GRANT MY SOLDIER GOD'S PERSPECTIVE

★  ★  ★

"The only true wisdom is in knowing you know nothing."

*Socrates*

*Dear Lord,* please open my soldier's eyes so he can see You at work around him. I know everywhere he turns the circumstances are tragic and overwhelming. I am afraid he is struggling to make sense of everything he's experiencing and not having much success. The large piece of the puzzle that he's missing is You, God.

Let him not just look at circumstances but, instead, begin to see the situation through Your eyes. I know You're working all around him and even through him, but he might not able to see that. Let him see beyond the physical and into the spiritual and catch a glimpse of Your plan. Give him reason to believe in Your love. I know You are trustworthy; please protect and restore his faith.

Don't let him be overtaken by discouraging thoughts. Put people in his life to give him the perspective he needs. And don't let people in his life who would reinforce the lies he may be believing. Show him that what he's doing has meaning and that his sacrifice makes a difference in the world in a good way. Heal his wounded and aching heart. Amen

★  ★  ★

*"And to man He said, 'Behold, the fear of the Lord, that is wisdom, and to depart from evil is understanding.'"*

*Job 28:28 NKJV*

# THANK YOU FOR A FIRM FOUNDATION

* * *

"You are not fighting for victory…you are fighting from victory!
Victory is already yours."

*Priscilla Shirer*

*Dear Lord,* it would be so easy to take for granted everything You do for us. At least it would if life weren't such a challenge right now. Right now I'm in a battle against the fear I feel for my soldier serving so far away. It would be so easy to be shaken by recent events, except that You have provided me with a firm foundation.

I don't have to be swayed by current events and disasters. I can be quietly confident that no matter what I see happening around the world, You are still in control. There is nothing that is too big or too horrible for You.

I know that even as You comfort me with this knowledge, it holds true for my soldier. No matter what she's facing, Your firm foundation will keep her safe. At times her world may seem to spin out of control, threatening to dislodge her from his faith. But Your foundation cannot be shaken. Neither can anyone who stands on that foundation.

You have provided us a solid place, secure from anyone or anything that would seek to cause us harm. Amen

* * *

*And they remembered that God was their rock, and the Most High God their Redeemer.*

*Psalm 78:35 NASB*

# KEEP MY SOLDIER GROUNDED IN YOUR TRUTH

★   ★   ★

"The truth does not change according to our ability to stomach it."

*Flannery O'Connor*

*Dear Lord,* I know how hard it is for me to stay focused on You, and I'm not in the middle of a war zone. Please keep my soldier grounded in Your truth. Give him like-minded friends to pray with. Help him find a group of other soldiers who want to study the Bible together.

Bring Scriptures to the forefront of his mind. Let him constantly be aware that You're there with him. Show him—in concrete, physical ways—that Your character isn't in conflict with what he's experiencing.

Make him yearn to spend time reading the Bible. When he opens to a page, let those verses jump out at him with instant application. Show him the relevance of Your Word to what is going on around him.

I know of so many soldiers who have come back angry at You because of what they've seen. Please protect him from that. Help him process what he's seeing. Let everything he experiences be reconciled with what he knows about You. Amen

★   ★   ★

*Sanctify them by the truth; your word is truth.*

*John 17:17 NIV*

# MAKE THE PLANS OF THE ENEMY OBVIOUS

★ ★ ★

"As you confront your problems rather than avoid them,
your faith is nurtured and stretched.
Your confidence grows; your fears subside."

*Charles Stanley*

*Dear Lord,* I know my loved one is doing an incredibly diffi-cult job, under tough circumstances. Make sure she can discern the plans of the enemy. Don't let her be caught unaware. I know that so often the enemy can hide in plain sight, pretending to be a friend. Make the hearts of those close to her clear so she will know who are friends and who are enemies.

Give her Your eyes, so she can read the body language and hear their intent in the tone of their voice. Give her the gift of discern-ment and anticipation while she's in the field so that she can know the plans of the enemy before they can carry them out. Don't allow her to be taken in by any who seek to deceive.

Keep her from any confusion or distractions while she's on pa-trol. When she travels, show her what lies in her path. Let any hid-den obstacles be obvious and easy to spot. Put other soldiers around her who also know the tricks and traps of the enemy. Help them work together to make sure all of them come home safely. Amen

★ ★ ★

*The Lord lifts up the humble; He casts the wicked down to the ground.*

*Psalm 147:6 NKJV*

# GOD PLEASE INTERVENE FOR MY SOLDIER

"Habits are first cobwebs, then cables.
The chains of habit are too weak to be felt
until they are too strong to be broken."

*Samuel Johnson*

★ ★ ★

*Dear Lord,* as my loved one fights a war half a world away, I pray You intervene for him and help him to be able to focus on the job at hand. Let him have time to evaluate his options when he's called on to make a choice. If he doesn't have the luxury of time, make sure his choices are clear and it's obvious which way he should turn.

Give him peace about the state of his loved ones at home. Don't let him worry about past situations, but to move forward in faith, knowing You are with him every step of the way.

Surround him with a hedge of protection as he faces enemies on all sides—those both seen and unseen. Inhabit the minds and foil the plans of all those who seek to hurt him and those he's protecting.

At the end of the day, when he's tempted to look back with regrets, give him the strength to turn those thoughts and questions over to You for safe-keeping. Touch him with Your wisdom, even as You touch him with Your protection. Amen

★ ★ ★

*Be very careful, then, how you live—not as unwise but as wise.*

*Ephesians 5:15 NIV*

# HELP MY LOVED ONE SEE GOD AT WORK

"Perfect goodness can never debate about the end to be attained,
and perfect wisdom cannot debate about
the means most suited to achieve it."

*C. S. Lewis*

★ ★ ★

*Dear Lord,* I'm praying for You to reveal Yourself to my loved one during this deployment. Give her the tools so she will do more than just get by, but have victories she never could have imagined.

Let her see glimpses of the way You work, and the way You love each of us with an unconditional abundance. Find ways to reinforce the lessons of discernment You're teaching her. Grow her faith in You and her faith in recognizing Your voice and the work You're doing around her.

As she goes about her daily life, drop moments of divine inspiration into her routine. Keep her actively looking for You everywhere, and then let her find You in the most unlikely places.

Use what she's learning to reach out to others and include her as You touch those who are hurting. Let her see the healing power of Your love and be a part of the work You're doing. Make her so aware of You that she never wants to stray from Your side. In all things, hold my loved one close and keep her safe. Amen

★ ★ ★

*I love those who love me, and those who seek me find me.*

*Proverbs 8:17 NIV*

# HELP MY SOLDIER UNDERSTAND WHAT HE SEES

*"Any fool can know. The point is to understand."*

*Albert Einstein*

★　★　★

*Dear Lord,* war is a horrible thing and the thought that my loved one is in the middle of it strikes fear into my soul. I know he's seeing things that are awful, but I pray he's also seeing how You are still Lord through tragic circumstances. Don't let him ignore the good You're doing around and through him.

I worry about the toll these experiences are taking on his mind. I know it would be so easy to get bitter and angry with all that's around him. But I also know You can protect him from that. Keep him, Lord, from becoming his own worst enemy.

He has such a tender heart and feels things so deeply. It's that heart to help others, to sacrifice, that made him willing to serve in the first place. But I worry his heart will be wounded beyond what he can bear. When circumstances get to be too much for him, help him turn to You. Give him what he needs to be able to process what he's seeing. Use those around him to help him sort through what he's experiencing and give him wise counsel and advice.

Most of all, bring him home whole and safe, as a stronger version of the person he was when he left. Amen

★　★　★

*Consider what I say, for the Lord will give you understanding in everything.*

*2 Timothy 2:7 NASB*

# GIVE MY SOLDIER DISCERNMENT

*"Life is just a series of trying to make up your mind."*

*Timothy Fuller*

★ ★ ★

*Dear Lord,* I'm asking You to be present in all the decisions my soldier has to make. She might be in a dark place right now, at the end of her own strength. It's time for You to step in and take over. Give her the clear head she needs to make wise decisions.

I know there are times when she has to make decisions with no time to consider all the facts, or when she'll never know all the facts but must go with her best guess. Don't let her decision rest in the flip of a coin, but in Your wisdom and all-knowing power.

Lend my loved one Your strength and clear away all confusion and distraction so she can see directly to the heart of the matter. Show her the things she needs even before she needs them. Only You can see everything clearly, and I know You can share that vision with her.

Her enemies can come at her anytime. Show her the truth of every situation where she finds herself. Don't let anyone deceive her, but make their true loyalties obvious.

Give her the confidence to make the hard decisions, and to rest on the things You've shown her. As the days go on, help her grow in faith as she comes to rely on You more and more. Amen

★ ★ ★

*Teach us to number our days, that we may gain a heart of wisdom.*

*Psalm 90:12 NIV*

# LET MY SOLDIER FIND JOY

★ ★ ★

"There is not a particle of life which
does not bear poetry within it."

*Gustave Flaubert*

*Dear Lord,* I know my loved one is experiencing things I can't even imagine. Just the phrase "horrors of war" strikes such fear in my heart for him. My prayer today is that he can look beyond his circumstances and find joy. Not the stuff that's fleeting but a deep abiding feeling that will carry him through the dark times.

Let him see the love we have for him here at home. Give him the certainty that what he's doing is for a greater good, even if at times it seems pointless. Show him that his sacrifice has meaning.

Let him see You at work around him. Surround him with friends and buddies. Let them laugh together, and spend time cutting up and, yes, even playing. Show him glimpses of the difference he's making in this world.

Surprise him with meaningful communication from home. Show him that he's not forgotten and instead is missed and already celebrated for the hero he is.

Lord, only You can accomplish these things, and although it scares me to ask, I believe You can do this. I know You love my loved one even more than I do, and You will honor this plea. Amen

★ ★ ★

*You give him blessings forever; You cheer him with joy in Your presence.*

*Psalm 21:6 HCSB*

# GIVE MY LOVED ONE
# CLEAR DIRECTION

★ ★ ★

"Eyes that look are common, eyes that see are rare."

*J. Oswald Sanders*

*Dear Lord,* I'm praying for my loved one to make wise choices while she's in a war zone. Give her insight into which way to turn whenever there's a fork in the road. Don't let her give in to temptation, but stay focused on doing what's right, no matter how difficult the choice is.

Put friends and mentors around her to help her navigate her path. I know she's facing difficult choices, and they're made even harder because she's tired and feels alone. Don't let momentary difficulties sway her to do something that will haunt her for a lifetime.

Protect my loved one when temptation is too much and always give her a way out of any situation, even if it is of her own making. Make her strong and willing to stand up for what's right, no matter who is opposing her. Keep her from the influence of those who would lead her astray. Make their company undesirable to her so she can't stand to even be around them.

In all things, remind her that You are with her and that no matter what happens, You will never leave her side. Amen

★ ★ ★

*I have directed you in the way of wisdom; I have led you in upright paths.*

*Proverbs 4:11 NASB*

# PRAISE FOR MY LOVED ONE'S WISDOM

★ ★ ★

"Honesty is the first chapter of the book wisdom."

*Thomas Jefferson*

*Dear Lord,* thank You for my loved one's wisdom. He has always shown great insight and discernment, no matter what situation he's facing. I know that's a gift from You, and it gives me so much comfort while he's far from home.

You've made him able to look at things honestly, no matter how difficult the situation where he finds himself. He's spent years walking closely with You, and I know you won't abandon him now. He's humble and knows how to ask for wisdom and listen to the counsel of others. You've surrounded him with good friends and given him commanders that have the experience to deal with what may come.

As I reflect on my soldier's life experiences, I know You've prepared him for this time in his life. He's equally able to pray through a decision or make a split-second choice because he's never far from You. Remind him that all wisdom comes from You, and don't let him wander from Your side. Amen

★ ★ ★

*Who is like the wise person, and who knows the interpretation of a matter? A man's wisdom brightens his face, and the sternness of his face is changed.*

*Ecclesiastes 8:1 HCSB*

# MAY MY LOVED ONE'S HOMECOMING BE JOYFUL

★ ★ ★

"The most wasted of all days is one without laughter."

*E. E. Cummings*

*Dear Lord,* as my loved one prepares to return home from her deployment, I pray for a sweet homecoming with family and friends. Don't let her arrival be delayed by mechanical issues or weather or even official red-tape. Keep her safe as she travels and then have people there to welcome her as she sets foot back on U.S. soil.

Don't let her homecoming be awkward in any way, but instead be filled with love and laughter and joy. Let her first few nights back home be easy, instead of stressful. Don't let her worry about living up to any expectations but only enjoy time with friends and family.

Use this homecoming to reinforce how much You love her and continue to heal her mind and erase the horrible things she's seen while she was at war. Keep her safe from nightmares and anxiety attacks. Don't let her get overwhelmed with visitors and crowds, but make sure she knows how much she was missed and how much her sacrifice means to all of us.

No matter what, let her know our love isn't dependent on her actions or anything else. Let her feel our joy of just being with her. Amen

★ ★ ★

*The Lord had done great things for us; we were joyful.*

*Psalm 126:3 HCSB*

# STRENGTH

Strength comes in many forms; physical, mental, even emotional. God can equip the ones we love to triumph over incredible circumstances, no matter what obstacles lie in their paths.

# GIVE MY LOVED ONE COURAGE

★   ★   ★

"If we desire our faith to be strengthened, we should not shrink
from opportunities where our faith may be tried,
and therefore, through trial, be strengthened."

*George Mueller*

*Dear Lord,* I know my loved one is encountering things she's
never had to deal with and never even seen before. Many of those
things may come with an overwhelming sense of fear. Protect her
from becoming immobilized by that fear.

Use this time to teach her to move forward no matter how
afraid she is. Surround her with honest friends who will open up
about their own fears and shortcomings and then let them encourage each other to new heights in Your name.

Let the fear she feels protect her from danger but never hinder
her when the situation calls for courage. Don't let the fact that she
feels fearful discourage her or make her feel inferior to those around
her. Instead show her that continuing to do the work she's been sent
to do, in the face of that fear, is the mark of true courage.

Give her the sense of accomplishment when she perseveres in
spite of the terror of the unknown. Always be with her, guiding her,
giving her strength and pouring Your love out on her. Amen

★   ★   ★

*Have I not commanded you? Be strong and of good courage; do not be
afraid, nor be dismayed, for the Lord your God is with you wherever
you go.*

*Joshua 1:9 NKJV*

# STRENGTHEN MY SOLDIER'S PRAYER LIFE

★ ★ ★

"God speaks to all individuals through what happens
to them moment by moment."

*J. P. DeCasssade*

*Dear Lord,* my soldier is a man of faith, and he trusts You with his life and with ours. He's always been a man who prays. Don't let the circumstances where he finds himself now change that. Keep him centered on You and on Your plan for his life.

While he's been gone, my prayer life has gotten stronger and stronger. I'm asking You to accomplish that in his life as well. Show him Your faithfulness to answer our prayers and to give us Your perspective on the things we don't understand.

Help him become so familiar with Your voice that he recognizes You in the mightiest roar or the tiniest whispered breeze.

Through these times of prayer make him more hungry to hear from You. Let him experience every aspect of prayer, from answers that come before the words leave our mouths to the abiding satisfaction of waiting to see You work through our perseverance. Make prayer second nature to him, showing him what it's like to have an ongoing conversation with You throughout every day. Amen

★ ★ ★

*Therefore I want the men everywhere to pray, lifting up holy hands without anger or disputing.*

*1 Timothy 2:8 NIV*

# LET MY LOVED ONE KNOW
# GOD'S LOVE

★ ★ ★

"He died not for men, but for each man. If each man had been
the only man made, He would have done no less."

*C. S. Lewis*

*Dear Lord,* make sure that my loved one knows how much You
love her. I know she's surrounded by the effects of war, and beyond
that, she's in a place where human life often has little or no value. In
the midst of these circumstances remind her how much You value
her. Remind her that You sacrificed everything for each of us as
individuals, and that each one is precious to You.

Help her reconcile the truth of Your love with what she sees
around her.

Lord, You can help her process all of this, and if not make sense
of it, at least come to peace with it. Put others around her to help
her see the truth in the midst of everything.

It seems like the evil in this world is increasing more each day,
but help my loved one remember that Your plan will not be overcome. You will be victorious and that no sacrifice, no matter how
small, will be forgotten. Amen

★ ★ ★

*"What do you think? If a man owns a hundred sheep, and one of them
wanders away, will he not leave the ninety-nine on the hills and go to
look for the one that wandered off?"*

*Matthew 18:12 NIV*

# GIVE MY SOLDIER TIME TO LAUGH

★　★　★

"Life is worth living as long as there's a laugh in it."

*L. M. Montgomery*

*Dear Lord,* give my soldier plenty of opportunities to relax and have fun while he's away. I know a lot of what he does is stressful; make sure he has even more time to rest and recover than he does for work.

Don't let him feel guilty for taking time to laugh and play when he's away from us. Help him know we are fine here. We miss him so much, but we don't want him to be miserable any more than he would want us to be miserable.

Surround him with good friends who can help him shake off the stress and worry that comes with this deployment. Protect him from those who would drag him down and keep him thinking about only negative things.

When I communicate with him, help me to find things to share with him that make him laugh and bring back happy memories. Don't let our conversations be so serious and sad, but give us time to share the joy we each have found.

Make the days speed by for him, and bring him home safe. Amen

★　★　★

*For the kingdom of God is not eating and drinking, but righteousness and peace and joy in the Holy Spirit.*

*Romans 14:17 NASB*

# PRAISE FOR MY SOLDIER'S STRENGTH

★ ★ ★

*"The strongest of all warriors are these two—Time and Patience."*

*Leo Tolstoy*

*Dear Lord,* thank You for the strength You've given my loved one. She's always been a strong woman, and I know that strength is serving her well. I also know it's not just a façade, but a core of steel that has been forged through her experiences and her relationship with You.

I know she will have struggles while she's serving so far from home, and there will be times when she'll wonder if she has what it takes to see this through. When those doubts come, show her how You've prepared her for what she's now facing. Don't ever let her forget that her strength comes from You. Remind her of past struggles she's faced and how You've given her the strength she needed to come out victorious.

Let those around her see how Your strength becomes hers. Give her the boldness to tell others how she manages to cope so well, no matter what challenges she has to face.

Even on those days when my fear for her seems overwhelming, I will remember that You are there with her. You promise to be all we ever need, and today I'm choosing to believe that.

★ ★ ★

*"For I know the plans I have for you," declares the Lord, "plans to prosper you and not to harm you, plans to give you hope and a future."*

*Jeremiah 29:11 NIV*

# LIFT MY SOLDIER'S SPIRITS

★　★　★

"Joy is love exalted; peace is love in repose; long-suffering is love enduring; gentleness is love in society; goodness is love in action; faith is love on the battlefield; meekness is love in school; and temperance is love in training."

*Dwight L. Moody*

*Dear Lord,* I'm asking You to give my loved one hope today. I know he's overwhelmed with everything going on around him. Sometimes, I hear in his voice that he's losing hope.

Please lift his spirits and give him the hope he so desperately needs. Let those around him see his mood and work to help him overcome his sadness. Give him glimpses of the ultimate purpose behind his mission.

I know we can all find our hope in You. Bring things to his mind that he can look forward to and anticipate with joy. Change his perspective from looking back and looking around to looking up and looking forward. Don't let his discouragement or the discouragement of those around him drag him down.

Surprise him with beauty in unexpected places and laughter when he least expects it. Make the time go quickly, and keep those he loves from all harm. Protect him from the ugliness of war. Guard his mind with a hope that endures forever. Amen

★　★　★

*Let us hold unswervingly to the hope we profess, for he who promised is faithful.*

*Hebrews 10:23 NIV*

35

# KEEP MY LOVED ONE'S
# HOPE ALIVE

★　★　★

"It is often in the darkest skies that we see the brightest stars."
*Richard Paul Evans*

*Dear Lord,* I cannot imagine how difficult it is to keep hope alive in the midst of war. Yet that is exactly where my loved one is. I ask You to keep her hope alive, in spite of her circumstances.

I know what she's doing is exhausting for her mind, as well as her body. Lord, please give her reasons to stay hopeful. Don't let what she sees and experiences destroy her outlook.

Put things and people around her to raise her spirits and restore her hope. Let her see beyond where she is. Give her special moments that she knows come directly from You. You are her rock and her foundation. Surround her with people to remind her what she's doing has a purpose. And more, that the purpose is for good and not evil.

I remember my loved one's tender heart, and I ache for the wounds it now carries. Heal those, and remove all traces of any scars. The Bible reminds me You are the God who sees. Look down at my soldier and wrap her in Your love. Amen

★　★　★

*A man's steps are established by the Lord, and He takes pleasure in his way. Though he falls, he will not be overwhelmed, because the Lord holds his hand.*

*Psalm 37:23-24 HCSB*

# GIVE MY LOVED ONE
# REFRESHMENT

★　★　★

"To see a candle's light one must take it into a dark place."
*Ursula K. Le Guin*

*Dear Lord,* please give my loved one the rest he needs to get through this time. I know he's being pushed to his limit physically and emotionally. He's fighting on all fronts, from total exhaustion to total boredom. Just the range of his battles is exhausting to think about.

I know he's under tremendous stress, and I worry about the toll it's taking on him. Give him the refreshment, the outlets he needs to cope with what's happening around him. Give him friends to talk with who are coping with the same issues, and then help them see You in the midst of all of it.

You are the only one who is with him all the time. Let him know You're there. Hold him up when he's weak, and give him the tools he needs to survive. Let him renew his strength in quiet moments of the day and in the stillness of the night. Guard him at night when he sleeps so his rest is undisturbed. Let him see some good in all that's around him. Amen

★　★　★

*For You have been a refuge for me, a tower of strength against the enemy.*
*Psalm 61:3 NASB*

# KEEP MY SOLDIER SPIRITUALLY STRONG

★ ★ ★

"In the depth of winter, I finally learned that within me there lay an invincible summer."

*Albert Camus*

*Dear Lord,* keep my loved one strong. I know these circumstances are taking a horrible toll on her. She's exhausted mentally, physically, and spiritually. Her circumstances present nothing but hardship everywhere she turns, except when she turns to You.

Help her focus on You. Show her what it's like to depend on You for everything she needs. Provide the perfect rest when she's so tired she can't go on. Grant her perfect peace when she's emotionally exhausted and unable to cope with one more ugly sight. Fill her up spiritually so that she has the foundation to keep moving on.

Remind her of the ways You've promised to provide for her and the ways You have provided for her. When she's hurting, be there to comfort her, through others, through Your word in the Bible, and through the prayers we're all sending on her behalf.

When her situation becomes too much to bear, put people around her to share the load. Give her friends to talk with, to laugh with, and to cry with. Don't ever let her feel like she's alone because I know she's not. I know You're there with her, and I thank You for that. Continue to lift her up in all ways. Amen

★ ★ ★

*It is God who arms me with strength and keeps my way secure.*

*2 Samuel 22:33 NIV*

# GIVE MY LOVED ONE
# PHYSICAL STRENGTH

★ ★ ★

"The strength of a man consists in finding out the way
in which God is going, and going in that way too."

*Henry Ward Beecher*

*Dear Lord,* give my loved one the physical strength he needs to
get through this assignment. I can't imagine the hardships he's facing and I'm asking You to equip him to stay physically healthy. Keep
his muscles strong as he carries the equipment he needs. Strengthen
his arms and legs and keep them from any kind of injury.

Guard his back, as it bears so much of the weight. Give him
supportive places to rest so his spine isn't stressed and has the time
needed to recover. Especially keep his joints from showing the signs
of extreme wear. I know just the weight of his uniform, with all the
protective armor, can cause injury if it's not balanced correctly.

I also pray for his health. He's in a different climate, with different plants and animals. Keep him from any kind of allergic reactions. Make sure his lungs stay healthy so his body can get the
oxygen it must have to perform at peak efficiency.

You are the creator and designer of our bodies, and You Lord
know how best to care for us. Keep my loved one's body healthy and
bring him home safe. Amen

★ ★ ★

*You armed me with strength for battle; you humbled my adversaries
before me.*

*Psalm 18:39 NIV*

# PREPARE MY SOLDIER
# FOR HER ENVIRONMENT

★ ★ ★

"Success comes from preparation."

*E'yen A. Gardner*

*Dear Lord,* today I'm asking You to help my loved one acclimate to the environment where she's stationed. I know it's nothing like she's used to and that difference can take a huge toll on her physically as well as mentally.

There are extremes of heat and cold, as well as different environmental factors. All these could be an added burden that she just doesn't need. Please help her to make the transition quickly and without incident.

Give her body the supernatural ability to adapt to the extremes she's facing. Don't let her feel the effects, even though they're present. You are the one who designed her body, and I'm asking You to intervene and stand as a barrier between my loved one and what she's facing.

Make it so she doesn't even notice the difference in climate and weather, but feels as comfortable as if she were at home. Ensure that her uniform protects her from extremes in temperature and doesn't add more hardship to what her body is already fighting. Give her a comfortable place to rest when her day is done. Amen

★ ★ ★

*God gives me strength for the battle. He keeps my way secure.*

*Psalm 18:32 NIRV*

# GIVE MY LOVED ONE
# YOUR COURAGE

★ ★ ★

"Freedom lies in being bold."

*Robert Frost*

*Dear Lord,* my loved one is one of the bravest men I've ever known. Yet even he is facing fears beyond imagining. I know he's seeing some of the worst things mankind can do. Give him the courage he needs to stay strong, no matter what he's exposed to during this deployment.

Show him that true courage isn't the absence of fear but continuing on in spite of what he's feeling. Help him to bring to mind the training he's had when the fear threatens to overwhelm him into inaction. Then let him know it's You who is at work in his heart, providing all that he needs.

Give him friends who will admit to feeling afraid and bind them together to support each other. Bring to mind the Bible stories he's heard and help him apply those truths to his situation.

Grow his courage and teach him to turn to You for protection and for confidence no matter what he's facing. Amen

★ ★ ★

*For I am the Lord your God who takes hold of your right hand and says to you, Do not fear; I will help you.*

*Isaiah 41:13 NIV*

# GIVE MY SOLDIER
# INNER STRENGTH

★ ★ ★

"Be sure you put your feet in the right place, then stand firm."

*Abraham Lincoln*

*Dear Lord,* while my loved one is away at war I'm asking You to bolster her inner strength. I know she's always been a strong woman, but she's facing situations she's never encountered before and needs all the courage she can find. Grant her the kind of courage that comes from deep inside, the kind of courage only You can provide.

Give her the inner core of steel that comes from a heart that's 100 percent sold out for You. Encase her values and beliefs in an unbreakable shell.

As she faces situations and circumstances that try her to the breaking point, remind her that who she is never changes, and even more importantly who You are, God, never changes. Bring her back to the identity You've planted deep inside her, and renew her strength from that.

Keep Your hand on her at all times, and protect her from all she sees and experiences. No matter what she faces, always bring her back to the safety of Your love. Amen

★ ★ ★

*Surely God is my salvation; I will trust and not be afraid. The Lord, the Lord himself, is my strength and my defense; he has become my salvation.*

*Isaiah 12:2 NIV*

# YOU ARE STRONGER THAN ANY ENEMY WE WILL EVER FACE

★ ★ ★

"Don't magnify your problems, magnify your God...
he's got you covered."

*Tony Evans*

*Dear Lord,* sometimes I'm overwhelmed by the might of Your power. You are the creator of the universe, yet You have made Yourself available to us. You have called me Your child and set Yourself as my protector. It's almost more than I can wrap my mind around.

In this world, enemies come at us from all sides, and yet we are safe.

The enemies we face would have us believe that we are powerless, even weak, because we choose to rely on You. Our reliance on You isn't a weakness at all. When we call on You, our enemies melt before You. None can stand against One so great as You.

The power You wield on our behalf is tempered with a love so great. Our enemies are blind to the power of love. I pray You will remind my soldier of this as he faces battles so far from home. Stand in front of him, and guard him from behind.

★ ★ ★

*On the day I called, You answered me; You made me bold with strength in my soul.*

*Psalm 138:3 NASB*

# BE MY SOLDIER'S SECURITY

\* \* \*

"Peace comes in situations completely surrendered
to the sovereign authority of Christ."

*Beth Moore*

*Dear Lord,* You are my only security during this difficult time. Please be my loved one's security as well. Be so obvious in the situations around her that she turns to You automatically. Let her see You in moments of joy, in spite of the ugliness everywhere she turns.

I can only imagine how difficult it must be to look beyond the tragedy she sees everywhere she looks, but You can provide her with those glimpses of beauty. Use them to give her the assurance she needs to know You are still beside her.

You promise to never leave us, but I know there are times when my loved one feels so lost and alone. Put people around her who can remind her of Your love and constant care. Don't let her ignore the good You're doing around and through her. Please don't let her turn her back on You, no matter what she sees.

I worry about the toll these experiences are taking on her mind. I know it would be so easy to get bitter and angry with all that's around her. I also know You can protect her from that. Bring her back to me safe and whole. Amen

\* \* \*

*The works of His hands are truth and justice; all His instructions are trustworthy.*

*Psalm 111:7 HCSB*

# YOU ARE MY LOVED ONE'S STRENGTH

★ ★ ★

"Strength is the matter of the made-up mind."

*John Beecher*

*Dear Lord,* I know how tired my loved one is. I can't imagine how he's stayed strong for so long. I know he's tired physically, and he's tired mentally. He needs the strength to remain diligent to see this job through to the end. I know that You are close beside him, giving him what he needs to continue on.

As he comes to the end of his own strength, I can rest assured that You will give him Your strength. I know You will renew him to the point where he barely remembers being ready to collapse. You promise to be strong when we are weak. Show him just how powerful You are when he calls out to You.

Strengthen his arms and his legs, so he can finish the job he's been given to do. Work in his mind to make him alert and ready to go.

I know he relies on You. Be there for him. Lift him up and carry him through. Amen

★ ★ ★

*The Lord is my rock, my fortress and my deliverer; my God is my rock, in whom I take refuge, my shield and the horn of my salvation, my stronghold.*

*Psalm 18:2 NIV*

# USE MY SOLDIER TO STRENGTHEN OTHERS

★ ★ ★

"Have God make a message out of your mess."

*Joyce Meyer*

*Dear Lord,* while my soldier is away on this deployment, use her to strengthen those around her. She's a woman of faith, and I know that she's relying on You while she's away. She knows You'll keep us all safe while she's gone. Let others see her faith.

Give her opportunities to show what You've done in her life. Let the peace she feels be obvious to those around her, to the point that they want to know her secret. I know she's experiencing hardship and seeing horrible things, but keep her steadfast in her love for You.

When she has the chance to share Your love with others, use her words to reinforce her own foundational beliefs. When those around her question her faith, give her the answers You want her to say. Don't let her become discouraged by what she sees or by what others might say.

Grow my loved one's faith by giving her concrete examples of Your love and Your provision for her and for others around her. Amen

★ ★ ★

*Therefore encourage one another and build each other up, just as in fact you are doing.*

*1 Thessalonians 5:11 NIV*

# PROTECT MY LOVED ONE FROM DESPAIR

★ ★ ★

"Sometimes God allows what he hates
to accomplish what he loves."

*Joni Eareckson Tada*

*Dear Lord,* let my loved one see You today. I know he's overwhelmed with the ugliness of war and am afraid that it's causing him to doubt so many things he's always believed. Doubt can be good if it leads to a stronger faith. Make sure that's what is happening with my soldier. Don't let him give in to despair.

I know the Bible promises You will never leave us, and I'm asking You to make that fact so strong in his life he'll never doubt again. Give him glimpses of how all our lives are intertwined and connected through You.

Make Yourself so obvious there's no way he could explain You away. Today let him see just how deep Your love is. Drop moments of divine inspiration into his mind, reinforcing how active You are in his life. Most of all, remind him of how much You love him.

As my loved one recognizes You, give him the courage to share what he's seeing with others. Give them the community they need to build a stronger faith. Amen

★ ★ ★

*For since the creation of the world His invisible attributes, His eternal power and divine nature, have been clearly seen, being understood through what has been made, so that they are without excuse.*

*Romans 1:20 NASB*

# FAITH

Trying circumstances can deepen our faith—or destroy it. When we remain focused on God, a stronger faith is the result, and that's our prayer for those who serve.

# REPLACE MY SOLDIER'S FEAR WITH FAITH

★ ★ ★

"Faith is the very first thing you should pack in a hope chest."

*Sarah Ban Breathnach*

*Dear Lord,* I'm asking You today for special comfort for my soldier. I know he's battling fear as he serves his nation. The ugliness of war is all around him. He's surrounded by so much that I can't even comprehend.

Protect his mind from the images of all he's seeing and from the memories that are forming. Lift him out of the circumstances he's in, and show him the things going on around him that are good. Help him focus on You and on the way You're working in his life and the lives of those around him.

Don't let what he sees destroy his faith. Instead, use this time to grow his faith. Put people around him to help him process what he's seeing and experiencing. Let him feel Your presence constantly. Give him Your hand, and lead him through this time of danger.

Be there in a real way, giving him no reason to doubt Your love and Your protection. Give him a glimpse of his future, when he's back with his family, and finally safe at home. Give him the answers that point him to You. Be his foundation, and don't let him accept anything as truth unless it comes from You. Amen

★ ★ ★

*Now faith is the assurance of things hoped for, the conviction of things not seen.*

*Hebrews 11:1 NASB*

# YOU ARE WORTHY OF OUR FAITH

★ ★ ★

"The secret of the mystery is: God is always greater.
No matter how great we think Him to be,
His love is always greater."

*Brennan Manning*

*Dear Lord,* You are faithful and true. You are a God worthy of our faith. You never leave us alone to fend for ourselves. No matter how deep the valley of the shadow of death, You are always beside us.

You have proved Your love for us in ways too numerous to count. We are each precious to You, and You make that so abundantly clear.

When I think of all the times you've rushed to the aid of my soldier, I'm moved to tears. You protect her in ways that would be impossible for anyone else. I'm praying that today she's reminded of Your faithfulness and love.

When we find ourselves surrounded by enemies inside and out, You are there. When the world around us ceases to make sense and everything is hopeless, You are there. When we're too tired, physically and mentally, to go on, You are there lending us Your strength.

You are the creator of the universe, and yet You love each of us in such a personal way. Don't ever let me forget all you've done for us. Amen

★ ★ ★

*I called to the Lord, who is worthy of praise, and have been saved from my enemies.*

*2 Samuel 22:4 NIV*

# FILL MY LOVED ONE WITH HOPE

★ ★ ★

"If you have been reduced to God being your only hope,
You are in a good place."

*Jim Laffoon*

*Dear Lord,* give my loved one hope. I know that where he is, hope is in short supply. The ugliness of war surrounds him and must overwhelm him with the destruction he sees. Replace the despair that comes with these circumstances, and give him the attitude he needs to see this through.

I feel like it's so long until he's coming home, and the time must drag even more for him. I am sure he's tired and am afraid he is losing hope. Bring happy, encouraging memories to his mind. Then give him joy and help him look forward to coming home. Don't let him give in to the despair he's feeling.

Make the time go quickly. Give him friends to share his free time, and keep him from boredom. Let his down time be filled with instances of fun and even silliness. Then, on those days that drag, surprise him with packages and letters from home. Fill his heart with the voices of those he loves.

Let his dreams be filled with the anticipation of his homecoming, instead of the fear of what-if. Remind him that You're always with him, and fill him with the hope that can only come from You. Amen

★ ★ ★

*"But now, Lord, what do I look for? My hope is in You."*

*Psalm 39:7 NIV*

# LET MY SOLDIER SEE YOU AT WORK AROUND HER

★ ★ ★

"Faith begins where the will of God is known."
*Kenneth E. Hagin Sr.*

*Dear Lord,* it's so hard for me to have faith while my loved one is in harm's way. I know it's got to be even harder for her. But instead of giving in to despair or fear, grow her faith, just like You're growing mine.

Become so real to her that she recognizes You no matter where she is. Show her how real You are. Beyond that, let her see how active You are in her life and in the lives of those around her. Use this difficult time to grow her faith into a foundation that will never fail.

When the fear threatens to overwhelm her, bring instances of Your faithfulness to her mind. Replace that fear with a solid faith, built on the foundation of what You are doing in her life right now.

Then give her the courage she needs to share what she's learned with those around her. Let her be used to grow the faith of others. Fill her with an overwhelming sense of peace that can only come from the certain knowledge that You have everything well in hand, no matter how tragic the circumstances.

You are everything she needs right now; prove that to her in ways that last a lifetime. Amen

★ ★ ★

*So then faith comes by hearing, and hearing by the word of God.*

*Romans 10:17 NKJV*

# GIVE MY SOLDIER THE FAITH TO MAKE IT THROUGH

★ ★ ★

"Faith is confidence in the veracity of what God has said."

*Larry Huggins*

*Dear Lord,* I know my soldier is in the midst of the dreadfulness of war. He desperately needs faith to make it through, and so do I. Unless he can get Your perspective on the suffering surrounding him, I am afraid he'll be overwhelmed with despair. Even with faith, fighting despair is going to be a difficult battle. Give him what he needs to fight that battle and come out the other side victorious.

Instead of being shaken by his circumstances, use them to grow his faith. Let him see the situations around him as evidence of You at work in spite of this world. We live in an imperfect world, and it's so easy to blame You for all the bad things we see. Give him Your perspective.

Give him opportunities to see You bring good out of bad. Teach him what it means to have faith in the hard times, as well as the good. Most of all, prove that You love him and will never abandon him. Amen

★ ★ ★

*Yet those who wait for the Lord will gain new strength; they will mount up with wings like eagles, they will run and not get tired, they will walk and not become weary.*

*Isaiah 40:31 NASB*

# LET MY LOVED ONE SEE FAITH IN THOSE AROUND HER

★ ★ ★

*"This is what the past is for! Every experience God gives us, every person He puts in our lives is the perfect preparation for the future that only He can see."*

*Corrie ten Boom*

*Dear Lord,* surround my loved one with those who will strengthen her faith. I know she's a strong woman, but even a strong believer will face times of doubt. During those times, give her comrades of faith. Let their foundation of belief inspire her.

Use her fellow soldiers to remind her of Your steadfast character. Give her strong examples of godly men and women to follow when her own faith wavers. Make sure she has close friends that she can share her struggles with honestly.

Put commanders who rely wholly on You in charge of her unit. Let faith be a common topic of conversation. Keep her safe from anyone who would undermine her foundation of belief in You.

I know that You use others to speak to us, especially during times of doubt and difficulty. Speak to her clearly through the actions of those close to her. Most of all, show her that it's through difficulties that our faith is made strong. Amen

★ ★ ★

*Therefore do not be foolish, but understand what the Lord's will is.*

*Ephesians 5:17 NIV*

55

# GIVE MY SOLDIER FAITH
# IN TIMES OF TROUBLE

★ ★ ★

"Faith goes up the stairs that love has built and looks out
the windows which hope has opened."

*Charles H. Spurgeon*

*Dear Lord,* it's hard for me to have faith during this time of my
loved one's deployment. I know he's having an even more difficult
time. We both need You so much. I guess we always needed You; we
just didn't pay attention. Are You listening now? I know the Bible
says You are; I just need to have faith, and so does he.

Please show my soldier that You're there with him, that his
struggles are Your struggles. Assure him You will never leave him
no matter what.

Put people around to help him when he struggles. Let him
know that he's not alone, physically or spiritually. As his faith grows,
give him the courage and wisdom to help others cope in this difficult situation.

Give him hope in the darkest moments, from unexpected places. Let Your peace surround him, even when his circumstances are
the opposite of peace. Assure him of Your love, and let him feel the
love of all those here at home. I'm calling on You now, God, to be
his refuge and strength. Amen

★ ★ ★

*God is our refuge and strength, a helper who is always found in times
of trouble.*

*Psalm 46:1 HCSB*

# DON'T LET GUILT OVERWHELM
# MY SOLDIER

★　★　★

"Mistakes are the usual bridge between inexperience and wisdom."

*Phyllis Therous*

*Dear Lord,* my soldier would sacrifice herself for another without thinking. Her caring heart is one of the reasons I admire her so much. It's also a source of worry for me. I'm afraid she'll be overcome with all kinds of guilt from feeling like she's not doing enough, or that she didn't make the right decision.

Protect her from this kind of destructive guilt. Show her how You are working through her in a powerful and positive way. Also give her proof that You're the one who works things together for good. The results are Your responsibility, not hers.

I know she could begin to second-guess her actions and decisions. This could make her hesitate when she needs to act, and that could put her in harm's way. Guard her against this.

She's a sensitive woman and can't stand to see others hurt or injured. Don't let this trait lead her to believe lies about what she has or hasn't done. Keep her focused on You as she goes about her work, and don't let her despair when things get bad.

Wrap her in Your love. Guard her heart, and protect her mind, no matter what circumstances surround her. Amen

★　★　★

*The lot is cast into the lap, but its every decision is from the Lord.*

*Proverbs 16:33 NASB*

# THANK YOU FOR STRENGTHENING MY SOLDIER'S FAITH

★ ★ ★

"Life is a succession of lessons which must
be lived to be understood."
*Helen Keller*

*Dear Lord,* it's so hard to thank You for what my soldier is going through. At least it's hard until I see how strong his faith has become. This time of struggle has made him even stronger than he was before he left.

You have taken a difficult experience and used it to forge a man of steel. I love hearing from him and seeing all the ways You've given him wisdom and grace.

While he's faced some things that I don't even want to think about, I know You've taken those things and filtered them, using them to make him more like You. His capacity to love and extend mercy are something that can only come from You.

Instead of this experience making him hard and bitter, I'm watching him grow in tenderness and love. So as much as I would never wish anyone to go through what he's gone through, I can see how You've used it to make him stronger.

He's experienced You in a way that few have, and I know that has left him changed for the better. I pray that he never forgets the lessons he's learned. Amen

★ ★ ★

*Your faith will be tested. You know that when this happens it will produce in you the strength to continue.*

*James 1:3 NIRV*

# GIVE MY SOLDIER WHAT
# SHE NEEDS TO STAY FAITHFUL

★ ★ ★

"All I have seen teaches me to trust the Creator
for all I have not seen."
*Ralph Waldo Emerson*

*Dear Lord,* let my loved one see You today. I know she's in the middle of miserable circumstances and must be weary of all that she sees. She needs the encouragement that only Your presence can bring.

Help her replace the images of war with the sure knowledge of how You're even now at work in the world around her. She's far from home and everything she holds dear. At times she has to feel like all her friends have moved on without her.

Don't let her feel abandoned by You too. Remind her of how much she is loved by everyone she's left behind. Move in the hearts of those who love her to reach out to her today, and all the days she's away. Never let a day go by without Your and our love for her being obvious.

Remind her that You're still there and of how much You love her. Show up in an unusual circumstance or person, but make sure she knows it's You. Strengthen my loved one's faith by allowing her to see her life from Your perspective. Give her just what she needs to continue to stay strong. Amen

★ ★ ★

*But the Lord is faithful, and He will strengthen and protect you from the evil one.*

*2 Thessalonians 3:3 NASB*

# WRAP MY SOLDIER
# IN YOUR LOVE AND CARE

★ ★ ★

"Though our feelings come and go, God's love for us does not."

C. S. Lewis

*Dear Lord,* remind my loved one that he belongs to You. Don't let him lose sight of how precious he is to You. I know You love him even more than I do. Look for ways to show him that every single day.

It must be so hard to stay focused on You with everything that's going on around him, and with all that he sees every day. I know You can remind him that You are still there, walking this path with him. Wrap him so tightly in Your love that he can't help but know You're there.

When he's tempted to doubt how much You love him, put someone in his life to tell him differently. Use those around him to prove Your love and Your care. Every time circumstances threaten to overwhelm him, replace his despair with proof of Your power and Your protection.

On those days when he's sure he can't go forward, give him the strength he needs. Make him remember all the ways You've worked in his life and through his life. Don't let him give in to doubt, but use this time to show him how to remain focused on You. Amen

★ ★ ★

*The Lord is righteous in all his ways and faithful in all he does.*

Psalm 145:17 NIV

# GIVE MY SOLDIER
# THE COURAGE TO BELIEVE

★  ★  ★

"True faith means holding nothing back. It means putting
every hope in God's fidelity to His promises."

*Francis Chan*

*Dear Lord,* today I'm asking You to help my loved one remember
You're still in control, no matter what happens around her. Show
her that Your plans will not be defeated or even delayed. In the
midst of terrible circumstances it's so easy to lose sight of You. Don't
allow that to happen with her.

Don't let my loved one wander too far from You. Instead keep
her close, and protect her from the effects of what she sees and hears
every day. I know she's going to encounter those who believe all
kinds of lies about You. Replace those lies with truth, and set people
around her to reinforce the truth of who You are.

Give her the courage to believe You in spite of her circumstances. I know war brings out the worst in humanity. Use this time to
remind her of the best. Let her witness acts of kindness and love
even in her current situation. Show her how much You value her
sacrifice and that You will never abandon her.

Make it so that everywhere she turns she sees evidence of Your
plan unfolding and proof of Your great love for each of us. Amen

★  ★  ★

*Wait for the Lord; be strong and take heart and wait for the Lord.*

*Psalm 27:14 NIV*

# SHOW MY SOLDIER YOUR LOVE
# IN THE HARD PLACES

★　★　★

"He persists in loving us with unending, outrageous love."
*Francis Chan*

*Dear Lord,* You are still God, no matter what circumstances surround us. Remind my loved one of that while he's away at war. He's in a hard place, seeing the worst of the human race. Guard his heart, and don't let him be injured emotionally.

I know of so many soldiers who return home scarred from what they've seen. I believe that You can protect my loved one from that kind of injury just as easily as You can protect him from physical harm. Use every opportunity to remind him of Your loving-kindness and mercy.

Don't let those around him who have turned their backs on You influence my loved one against You. Keep him strong, and don't let his mind be filled with lies about You, God. He loves You; please don't let what he's experiencing make him abandon You.

When he experiences doubts, put people in his life to speak Your truth to him. Use others to remind him how much You love us and how the pain we experience hurts You as much or more than it hurts us. Show him Your love in the hard places. Amen

★　★　★

*God, who has called you into fellowship with his Son, Jesus Christ our Lord, is faithful.*

*1 Corinthians 1:9 NCV*

# FEED MY SOLDIER'S FAITH

★  ★  ★

"Faith does not eliminate questions.
But faith knows where to take them."
*Elisabeth Elliot*

*Dear Lord,* as my loved one goes about her duties, let her see You at work everywhere she turns. Never let her forget that it's You who is protecting her. Give her glimpses of You through the people she meets and in all her situations.

As much as she wants to be back home, let her find joy in her circumstances. Teach her how to be content no matter what is happening around her. Show her how this difficult time of service can be one that strengthens her faith and brings her closer to You.

Make my loved one aware of the role You play as her protector and guide. Help her when she's down. Let her hear from us here at home on a regular basis and make sure that all the packages and letters sent to her arrive safely and in good condition.

No matter what happens, let her see it from Your perspective. Don't let her be deceived into believing You don't care or have abandoned her. I know Your love for her knows no bounds, and I give thanks that You are watching over her day and night. Amen

★  ★  ★

*And the Lord said, "If you had faith like a mustard seed, you would say to this mulberry tree, 'Be uprooted and be planted in the sea'; and it would obey you."*

*Luke 17:6 NASB*

# LET MY LOVED ONE SEE YOU WALKING BESIDE HIM

★ ★ ★

"Faith is taking the first step,
even when you don't see the whole staircase."
*Martin Luther King, Jr.*

*Dear Lord,* I'm asking You to let my loved one see You walking beside him through all he experiences during this deployment. Never let him doubt Your presence. Show him how You're working in the circumstances around him, despite the ugliness of war everywhere he looks.

Use the situations that seem impossible to resolve, and show the power of Your love at work. I know it's easy to be overwhelmed with the tragedy around us; don't let that happen to the soldier I love and admire. Instead, as he goes through each day, make him aware of positive things happening around him, and don't let him dwell on the things that are negative.

I know You're working in his life right now. Give him opportunities to take part in positive, life-building work. Use him to build up the morale of those around him. Give him times of joy during this deployment, and let those overshadow the times of tragedy. Most of all show him the effect he can have on the people around him when he stays close to You. Amen

★ ★ ★

*The Lord replied, "My Presence will go with you, and I will give you rest."*

*Exodus 33:14 NIV*

# HELP MY LOVED ONE TRUST GOD'S CHARACTER

★ ★ ★

"When trouble comes, focus on God's ability to care for you."

*Charles Stanley*

*Dear Lord,* today I'm asking You to give my loved one a heart that is set on You. I know she's seen some horrible things during this war, and if those things have made her doubt that she knew You at all, then reconcile all that she's seen with who You are, God.

I know she's hurting because of all the death and injury she's seen. She's been exposed to the worst side of mankind. Show her how these horrible things were never Your plan but the result of our own choices as humans.

Give her the ability to glimpse Your perfect plan and the way You are bringing good out of a horrible situation. Even though we can't comprehend how a God of love can allow some of these things, give her the faith to accept Your love.

Don't allow bitterness to take root in my loved one's heart. Don't let the emotional wounds she's suffered from what she's seen fester and fill her heart with poison against You. Instead, heal her and give her the answers she needs.

No matter what, never give up on her, and never allow her to run too far from Your tender care. Amen

★ ★ ★

*Make sure that no one falls short of the grace of God and that no root of bitterness springs up, causing trouble and by it, defiling many.*

*Hebrews 12:15 HCSB*

# THANK YOU FOR
# YOUR STEADFAST LOVE

★ ★ ★

*"Here's the paradox. We can fully embrace God's love only when we recognize how completely unworthy of it we are."*

*Ann Tatlock*

*Dear Lord,* I love You so much. As much as I love You, I know You love me even more. You would pay any price to make sure I'm safe. Within the confidence of that truth, I also know that You love my soldier.

Armed with that knowledge, I can be at peace, knowing You will care for him no matter what happens. I hear about all that's going on around him, and it's so tempting to give in to fear. Then I remember that he can never leave the protection of Your love.

There's nowhere too dangerous, nowhere too remote, nowhere too dark to separate us from Your love. Everywhere I look I see the evidence of Your great love.

All of this is true for my soldier as well. You've put people around him to be there when he needs them. They encourage him, support him, and protect him. You don't love us in a vacuum. Creation itself is a reflection of Your great love. Amen

★ ★ ★

*For I am persuaded that not even death or life, angels or rulers, things present or things to come, hostile powers, height or depth, or any other created thing will have the power to separate us from the love of God that is in Christ Jesus our Lord!*

*Romans 8:38-39 HCSB*

# LET MY SOLDIER SEE
# THE DIFFERENCE SHE MAKES

★　★　★

"We may ignore, but we can nowhere evade the presence of God.
The world is crowded with Him. He walks everywhere incognito."

*C. S. Lewis*

*Dear Lord,* I know this time of deployment is incredibly hard on
my loved one. I wouldn't wish it for her if I had a choice. But I'm
asking You to take this and use it to grow her faith in You.

Show her the eternal significance of what she's doing. Show her
how it affects not just her but so many others. Use this time to prove
Your love in difficult circumstances. Help her to come to an understanding of who You are and how perfect Your plan is for each of us.

Let her see that nothing horrible can interfere with the ultimate
purpose You have. Help her reconcile You as the God of love with
the God who has allowed wars and other tragedies to occur. This
isn't something any of us can put into words, but I know You can
give her a peace about this seemingly irreconcilable difference.

Teach my loved one to walk in faith and not rely on a more
limited point of view. Give her a glimpse of Your point of view and
how deep and how wide Your love truly is, no matter what happens
around her. Amen

★　★　★

*Whether you turn to the right or to the left, your ears will hear a voice
behind you, saying, "This is the way; walk in it."*

*Isaiah 30:21 NIV*

# RENEW MY LOVED ONE'S FAITH IN YOU

★ ★ ★

"Never be afraid to trust an unknown future to a known God."

*Corrie ten Boom*

*Dear Lord,* I'm praying that my loved one will not turn his back on You because of what he's seeing during this war. I can only imagine the circumstances he's in right now. I know his life growing up hasn't prepared him for the incredible tragedy of war. He's going to have to fight to reconcile what he thought the world was like with what he's experiencing right now. I know that's where the danger lies. It's going to be hard for him not to become bitter and cynical, and even harder not to blame You.

Whatever it takes, remind him that You are the same yesterday, today, and tomorrow. Show him Your love, and help him to see Your purpose behind the ugliness all around him. I know You are a God of love and mercy and justice.

Give him a glimpse of the eternal significance of what's happening around him. Let him see how You work outside of time to bring good out of bad. Renew his confidence in You, and remind him that You are not indifferent to the suffering all around him. Let him see the hurt in Your heart at the condition of the world and how Your plan will someday make everything new. Amen

★ ★ ★

*For the Lord will be your confidence and will keep your foot from being caught.*

*Proverbs 3:26 NASB*

# INSTILL CONFIDENCE IN THOSE AROUND HER AND IN HERSELF

★ ★ ★

"Faith is a living, daring confidence in God's grace, so sure and certain that a man could stake his life on it a thousand times."

*Martin Luther*

*Dear Lord,* give my loved one the confidence she needs. The responsibility she must feel is something I can't begin to imagine. Protect her from taking on things that aren't hers. Her sense of responsibility is one of the things I value in her. Don't let it become a burden and a liability in this situation.

Don't let her begin to doubt those around her. Give her reasons to trust their judgment and their choices. Surround her with wise friends who will instill confidence. Give her commanders insight into what is best for those who serve below them.

Safeguard her mind from doubts about herself. Don't let her fall victim to second-guessing the split-second decisions she's had to make. Show her how You've used her to affect those around her in a positive way.

Most of all, don't let her doubt You, God. Show her how You work through her to bring about Your purpose. Give her the wisdom to cry out to You when she doesn't know which way to turn. Remind her that, ultimately, everything rests in Your hands. Amen

★ ★ ★

*The sum of Your word is truth, and every one of Your righteous ordinances is everlasting.*

*Psalm 119:160 NASB*

# TEACH MY SOLDIER
# TO RELY ON YOU

★ ★ ★

"There are no 'if's' in God's world. And no places that are safer
than other places. The center of His will is our only safety—
let us pray that we may always know it!"

*Corrie ten Boom*

*Dear Lord,* I know, beyond a shadow of a doubt You're all I need.
I'm asking You to make that truth real in my loved one's life.

His training has shown him how to rely on himself, on his comrades, and on his commanders. While he's away, teach him how to
rely on You. Lead him step-by-step into such a solid relationship
with You that You're the first person he turns to in every circumstance of life.

Become a foundation in his life that will never shift, never
shake, and never collapse. Help him build on that foundation and
become an even stronger version of the man who left to serve his
country. He's a proud, tender warrior. Give him the ability to rely
totally on You so You can accomplish all You want in his life.

Don't let him fall for the lie that relying on You is weak. Instead,
give him examples of strong people he respects who also rely on
You. Become the strongest part of his life. Amen

★ ★ ★

*But seek first his kingdom and his righteousness, and all these things will
be given to you as well.*

*Matthew 6:33 NIV*

# GIVE MY SOLDIER FAITH IN THE MIDST OF EVIL

★ ★ ★

*"Faith is not the belief that God will do what you want.*
*It is the belief that God will do what is right."*
*Max Lucado*

*Dear Lord,* I'm praying for my loved one's faith today. I know it's got to be shaken by what she's seeing around her. Instead of being shaken, use her circumstances to strengthen her faith. Let her see the situations around her as evidence of Your great love.

We live in an imperfect world. Let her see evidence of how You work things together for good, instead of for evil. Use the situations around her to strengthen her faith in ways that will prepare her for the future You have for her.

Lord, I can't begin to imagine how You can do that in the middle of a war zone, but I'm asking You to show up in a mighty way. I know that in the Bible there are stories of horrible circumstances, yet people could see You at work. They could watch You bring good things out of bad situations.

Let my loved one see how great You are and how You still perform miracles. Give her evidence that You still show up when You are called. Renew her faith and make her stronger. Amen

★ ★ ★

*We know that all things work together for the good of those who love God: those who are called according to His purpose.*

*Romans 8:28 NASB*

# PROTECTION

This world can be a scary place, especially when a loved one is serving half a world a way. God can provide the protection we can't and cover us all with the gift of peace.

# PROTECT MY SOLDIER
# AS HE LEAVES FOR WAR

★ ★ ★

"Basically, there are two paths you can walk: faith or fear.
It's impossible to simultaneously trust God and not trust God."

*Charles Stanley*

*Dear Lord,* my loved one is leaving for war, and I'm scared for him. I'm fearful he'll be injured or, worse, won't return at all. I know there's a lot involved with getting him to the actual battle zone, and even that scares me.

He'll be on numerous trucks, buses, and airplanes, and any of them could have a problem and he could be hurt. That's what I'm concentrating on right now. I'm asking You to protect him as he travels to the places he'll be stationed during this war.

Go before him and make his way there safe. Make sure the mechanics and those in charge of all his travel vehicles are diligent to go over every part and make certain they are travel worthy. Keep any enemies from having any contact with these methods of transportation.

Don't allow weather or any kind of environmental factor to expose him to danger while he travels. Keep him safe as he settles in, and then bring him back to his family whole and uninjured. Amen

★ ★ ★

*"The Lord himself goes before you and will be with you; he will never leave you nor forsake you. Do not be afraid; do not be discouraged."*

*Deuteronomy 31:8 NIV*

# THANK YOU FOR THE PROTECTION YOU PROVIDE MY SOLDIER

★  ★  ★

"You always have God's undivided attention."
*Charles Stanley*

*Dear Lord,* I know that as much as I love my soldier, You love her even more. You are faithful beyond my ability to understand. Thank You for the protection I know You're providing her.

When I find myself worrying about all the things she's experiencing, I remember that You are there with her. You are her shield. You are her closest confidant, and You hear the cries of her heart.

Let her see evidence of Your love and care as she travels through her days. Put reminders in her path so she can grow in her confidence and faith. And remind me that before I ask, You've already provided everything she needs.

It's hard for me to sit here, safe, when I know the challenges she faces. Remind me that Your plans for each of us are for good, not evil. Use this time to make each of us stronger. Allow us to experience Your love in a way we never imagined. Amen

★  ★  ★

*My God is my rock. I go to him for safety. He is like a shield to me. He's the power that saves me. He's my place of safety. I go to him for help. He's my Savior. He saves me from those who want to hurt me.*

*2 Samuel 22:3 NIRV*

# BE MY SOLDIER'S SHIELD

★  ★  ★

"Anything under God's control is never out of control."
*Charles R. Swindoll*

*Dear Lord,* I know how hard this deployment is on my loved one. But in spite of that, I'm praying for You to use these difficulties to make Yourself even more real in his life. Help him to meet You in ways he'd never have had the opportunity to if he'd stayed safe at home. Show him things he never imagined, things he can't explain except through You.

I never want to think of my loved one in harm's way, but I know You can use this time to stretch him and grow him into the man You've always planned for him to be. Keep him close to You, and don't let him use the ugliness of what he sees to reject You. Guard his mind, and when necessary be a shield keeping him from sights and experiences that would harm him.

Show him how good can come from bad times and bad situations. Let him have experiences that will strengthen him for the trials he still has to face in this lifetime. Let him see Your sorrow at the world where we live. Help his heart to become more like Yours, and no matter what, don't let him separate himself from You. Amen

★  ★  ★

*But you, Lord, are a shield around me, my glory, and the One who lifts my head up high.*

*Psalm 3:3 NIV*

# PROTECT MY LOVED ONE
# FROM GUILT

★  ★  ★

"No mind, no wisdom—temporary mind, temporary wisdom—
eternal mind, eternal wisdom."

*Adoniram Judson*

*Dear Lord,* no matter what happens, protect my loved one from guilt. I worry about how she'll react if something tragic happens. I've heard of survivor's guilt, and I know this is a danger all our men and women in the military face. But my loved one's in the middle of a war, and I know she's going to witness tragedy, if she hasn't already. Prepare her now to cope with that kind of emotional stress.

I know when something bad happens we tend to feel like there's always something more we could have done. But don't let her give in to that mindset. Whatever the situation, show her the truth of what really happened and don't let her dwell on the what-ifs. She's got such a tender heart; I know she'd rather be injured than watch someone else be hurt.

Help her turn to You with her feelings of guilt, then take those feelings away from her. Walk with her through this emotional minefield and keep her from self-destructing. Only You can repair a heart that's torn apart. Amen

★  ★  ★

*With it he touched my mouth and said, "See, this has touched your lips; your guilt is taken away and your sin atoned for."*

*Isaiah 6:7 NIV*

# PROTECT MY SOLDIER FROM BECOMING BITTER

★ ★ ★

"Bitterness imprisons life: love releases it."

*Harry Emerson Fosdick*

*Dear Lord,* I worry about the toll this deployment is going to have on my loved one's mind. I hear so much about soldiers who return home angry, bitter, or worse. Please protect him from that kind of an injury. Keep him safe spiritually and emotionally. Don't let what he sees while he's away make him doubt You.

I worry that he could get so despondent with what he's experiencing that he turns his back on You. Protect him from that. Make sure that each day he sees the good You're doing all around him. Let him also see how You are using him to make a positive difference in the world.

I know none of us can fully understand how such horrible things as war can exist in a world that You inhabit. But I do know You are trustworthy. We can place our faith in You and know we have a firm foundation. Don't let my loved one's foundation be shaken to the point where he comes home empty, believing in nothing.

Keep him in perfect peace so he can be an instrument of change, instead of giving up on You. Amen

★ ★ ★

*Get rid of all bitterness, rage and anger, brawling and slander, along with every form of malice.*

*Ephesians 4:31 NIV*

# PROTECT MY SOLDIER FROM HER ENEMIES

★  ★  ★

"Worry is a cycle of inefficient thoughts
whirling around a center of fear."

*Corrie ten Boom*

*Dear Lord,* protect my loved one. I'm so afraid she's in danger. I know there are people trying to kill her, and I can't even wrap my mind around that fact. I beg You to protect her. Give her supernatural wisdom as she goes about her duty. Let her see the hidden dangers in her path.

At times I can almost feel her enemies hunting her, and it scares me so much. I know You can keep her safe. I've always tried to protect her, and now she's half a world away and I'm powerless. But You promise that You are able to protect those who seek You.

Give her the insight she needs to stay safe. Guard those around her, and protect them as well. Show her commanders the plans of the enemy; make their conniving transparent and easy to spot. Protect her from the poor judgment that comes when she's tired or just not paying attention.

Confuse the enemy, and let their plans fall to pieces. Don't allow them to triumph in even a small thing. Make them discouraged, and overwhelm them with Your presence. Amen

★  ★  ★

*In God I have put my trust, I shall not be afraid. What can man do to me?*

*Psalm 56:11 NASB*

# SEND YOUR ANGELS TO GUARD
# MY LOVED ONE

★ ★ ★

"Our truest nature is to help others, and to protect and love them.
We care about others, and delight in seeing others happy and safe."

*Bryant McGill*

*Dear Lord,* I want more than anything for my loved one to be
safe. I long for the days when we were together, when I could protect him. I'm so proud of the man he's become, but it frightens me
that I can't be there to keep him from harm.

Now I'm turning him over to You. I know You've always been
there. But even though I know You'll protect him, it scares me that
I'm not in control. Instead, I'm miles away. I want to be there physically, to shield him. And not just from the physical dangers but also
from the harm I know that comes to his heart and mind.

Some days I worry more about his heart and mind than anything else. I hear of so many soldiers with problems after they come
home, and for years afterward. Please God, protect him from that
kind of trauma. Guard his mind and his heart. Keep them whole
and intact.

I know from the Bible that You sometimes send Your angels to
stand guard around someone. Please send them to protect my loved
one. Keep him safe from anyone or anything that would bring him
harm. Amen

★ ★ ★

*The Lord will protect you from all harm; He will protect your life.*

*Psalm 121:7 HCSB*

# GUARD MY SOLDIER'S REST

★ ★ ★

"Every outcome of every challenge should reveal how God supplies the grace to make it through the seemingly impossible."

*Father Leo Patalinghug*

*Dear Lord,* I know I've had trouble sleeping while my soldier is away, and I'm still in my familiar and comfortable bed. It must be so much harder for my loved one to get enough rest. She needs to stay strong so she can stay safe. Guard her rest, and make sure she gets enough sleep to stay focused during the day.

Don't let her dreams be littered with nightmares and restlessness. Instead, grant her deep sleep that renews her mind. I know her bed is hard and uncomfortable, but I'm asking You to make it feel like it's as familiar as her place at home.

Wrap her in Your protection as she sleeps, and keep the enemy from attacking her. Let those who stand guard have the insight to know the plans of the enemy and defeat them at every turn. When it's her turn to stand guard, multiply the rest she's had so she can stay alert and ready for anything that comes.

Wherever she lays her head, be there with her. Comfort her with Your peace, and reassure her of Your love. Amen

★ ★ ★

*Those who go to God Most High for safety will be protected by the Almighty.*

*Psalm 91:1 NCV*

# PROVIDE DELIVERANCE FOR MY LOVED ONE

★  ★  ★

*"The best way to find out if you can trust
somebody is to trust them."*

*Ernest Hemingway*

*Dear Lord,* I'm praying right now for deliverance for my loved one. I feel like there's something going on at this very minute, and I'm asking You to intervene on his behalf. Stand between him and anyone or anything that means him harm, whether it's physical or otherwise.

Give my loved one and those around him supernatural insight into where all danger lies. Let them anticipate the traps their enemies have set. Confuse his enemies, and make them weak so they cannot carry out their plans.

Lord, You are able to see everything, and I'm praying You will turn Your eyes on my soldier and guard him. Don't let anything happen to him or to those around him. Call in Your angels, and set them as guards along the paths he'll be taking.

Let him see You at work as You guard him and keep him safe. Give him confidence in You so that no matter what happens, he turns to You first. Show him Your great love and Your perfect peace. Amen

★  ★  ★

*Bow down Your ear to me, Deliver me speedily; Be my rock of refuge, A fortress of defense to save me.*

*Psalm 31:2 NKJV*

# PROTECT MY SOLDIER'S FAITH DURING THE DIFFICULT TIMES

★ ★ ★

"Every experience God gives us, every person he brings into our lives, is the perfect preparation for the future that only he can see."

*Corrie ten Boom*

*Dear Lord,* there are times when I worry about my loved one's faith. I know she's seeing some awful things, and I worry that she'll become bitter and angry toward You. Keep her heart firmly fixed on You. Don't let what she's experiencing overshadow what she knows about You.

Give her more times of joy than there are times of stress and sorrow. Don't let any bad memories take hold and return to haunt her after she comes home. Replace any of those memories with the certainty that You're still at work and things haven't spiraled out of Your control.

Remind her of Your power and love. Show her how You protect those who cannot protect themselves. Use her to provide that protection so she will have a clear vision of why she's there and the work she's supposed to do. Above all, keep her safe and bring her home soon. Amen

★ ★ ★

*The Lord is my strength and my shield; my heart trusts in Him, and I am helped; therefore my heart exults, and with my song I shall thank Him.*

*Psalm 28:7 NASB*

# PROTECT MY LOVED ONE
# FROM TROUBLE

★ ★ ★

"Talk we will of faith, if we do not trust and rely upon Him,
we do not believe in Him."

*Anthony Farindon*

*Dear Lord,* I'm once again praying for You to protect my loved one while he serves. I know that there are times when he can get himself into trouble. It only takes a moment of poor choices to give his commanders reason to discipline him.

I know that boredom can be a great threat. Don't let him or his fellow soldiers give in to temptations that can lead them astray.

Tonight I'm asking You to keep him away from trouble. Keep him from others who are foolhardy and don't think before they act. I know this is a small thing, but I also know that You care about the things that Your children care about. Keep a close watch on him as he goes about his duties, and especially as he fills his free time.

No matter what he and his buddies are up to, make sure they turn to You for their protection, relying on Your wisdom and on the tools You have given them for the job they have to do. Amen

★ ★ ★

*I waited patiently for the Lord; he turned to me and heard my cry. He lifted me out of the slimy pit, out of the mud and mire; he set my feet on a rock and gave me a firm place to stand.*

*Psalm 40:1-2 NIV*

# CONFOUND AND CONFUSE MY LOVED ONE'S ENEMY

\* \* \*

"Fear tries to get us to give up, but faith takes us
all the way through to victory."

*Joyce Meyer*

*Dear Lord,* I'm asking You to intervene and thwart all the plans the enemy has against my loved one and against all our military. I'm asking You to curse them with confusion and indecision. And I pray for You to make their leaders ineffective. Keep their weapons from working properly and their vehicles in disrepair. Burden them with frustrations so intense they want nothing more than to desert. And give them an overwhelming fear of our troops.

Make it impossible for them to carry out their plans. Sow seeds of distrust and disloyalty within their ranks, causing their soldiers to retreat instead of attack. Cause their communication to break down so one person doesn't know what another is doing.

Incite rebellion, and make them doubt the goals their leaders have set. Most of all, make the plans of the enemy obvious to all our troops. Make those who would harm my loved one clumsy and easy to spot. No matter what, guard and protect our brave men and women in the military. Amen

\* \* \*

*But You have saved us from our enemies, and have put to shame those who hated us.*

*Psalm 44:7 NKJV*

85

# I KNOW YOU SURROUND MY SOLDIER WITH ALL THE PROTECTION SHE NEEDS

★ ★ ★

*"No matter what you're going through there's no pit so deep that God can't reach in and get you out."*

*Joyce Meyer*

*Dear Lord,* it's so hard to have someone I love in danger. It would be an impossible situation if I didn't know You were watching over her. I know that You go before my soldier, providing a safe path for her. You also stay close behind her, protecting her from any who attack from behind.

You know the beginning from the end. When calamity strikes, You are able to take what seems like tragedy and make it into a blessing.

Your protection extends to the height and breadth and width of the earth. There is no place above or below where You cannot keep us safe. Our enemies cannot penetrate Your defense. They are forced into a war of deception and deceit,

Renew my soldier's hope. Remind her that You are all the protection she needs. You are faithful and will never abandon her or forsake her. Amen

★ ★ ★

*Do not fear, for I am with you; do not be afraid, for I am your God. I will strengthen you; I will help you; I will hold on to you with My righteous right hand.*

*Isaiah 41:10 HCSB*

# GO BEFORE MY SOLDIER

★ ★ ★

"A man of courage is also full of faith."

*Marcus Tullius Cicero*

*Dear Lord,* I'm so proud of my loved one and his willingness to serve in the military. But I'm afraid his spirit of sacrifice will put him in danger. So I'm asking for special protection for him. Help him fulfill the plan of becoming all You mean him to be, but also keep him from foolhardy actions.

As a soldier, he will not consider himself when someone else is in danger, and I know that is why he is a good soldier. Go before him and keep him safe. When he dashes into danger without thinking, cover him with Your protection.

Give him insight into the dangers that hide around him and around those he's with. Let him be the man You made him, but with an added degree of caution and care. Don't let his tendency to rush in put others in danger as they move to protect him as well.

Help him learn to evaluate every situation and see it from Your viewpoint. Equip him well to serve in this situation, always keeping Your hand on him. Amen

★ ★ ★

*You are my hiding place; you will protect me from trouble and surround me with songs of deliverance.*

*Psalm 32:7 NIV*

# BE WITH MY SOLDIER
# AS SHE SLEEPS

★ ★ ★

"True silence is the rest of the mind; it is to the spirit
what sleep is to the body, nourishment and refreshment."

*William Penn*

*Dear Lord,* I'm worried that my loved one isn't getting enough
rest. I know how hard it is to be in a strange place, without the comfort of home. Help her cope with all these challenges so she can be
rested and ready to face the battles she has in front of her.

Keep the nightmares far from her while she sleeps. Give her
the ability to sleep anywhere and to drop immediately into a deep
resting sleep. And on the nights when she doesn't get enough rest,
multiply what she does get so she's able to stay alert while she's on
patrol.

I know she also needs the time for emotional release so she can
relax and be ready for sleep. Provide that for her. Give her friends
to share fun and laughter with. Keep the enemy far from where she
lays her head at night.

Don't let her be burdened with us at home. Give her the assurance she needs to release the worry she feels for us. In all things,
surround her with Your perfect peace. Amen

★ ★ ★

*"Come to me, all of you who are tired and have heavy loads, and I will
give you rest."*

*Matthew 11:28 NCV*

# MAKE THE ENEMY UNSUCCESSFUL

★ ★ ★

"Faith activates God—fear activates the enemy."

*Joel Osteen*

*Dear Lord,* You see everything, know everything that is going to happen. Please protect my loved one from the enemy.

Intervene by making his enemies unsuccessful in everything they attempt. Make them clumsy and obvious when they try to hide or infiltrate places that should be safe. Curse them with confusion, and set up situations when they mistrust each other and their own leaders.

Don't let their weapons work but instead fall apart when used. Give them leaders who are harsh and unthinking. Don't let them know the plans of our soldiers. Keep them in constant misery, always uncomfortable and never able to rest.

Show them the worst in their leaders. Allow them so much frustration that all they want to do is give up and walk away. Then cover them with an overwhelming fear and knowledge that they cannot ever find victory through this path.

Allow our own soldiers victory over the enemy at every turn, keeping our brave men and women safe. Amen

★ ★ ★

*Lord, even when I have trouble all around me, you will keep me alive. When my enemies are angry, you will reach down and save me by your power.*

*Psalm 138:7 NCV*

# YOU ARE A GOD WHO IS MIGHTY AND ABLE TO SAVE

★ ★ ★

"Why do so many Christians pray such
tiny prayers when their God is so big?"

*Watchman Nee*

*Dear Lord,* I know You are powerful, wise, and able to save. As my mind roils with images of where he might be and what he's facing, my heart falters. Then I remember the power of the God we serve, and I am comforted.

Your Name is the one above all names, and You have given Your children the authority to call on You. You are never too busy and never too preoccupied.

There is nothing that our enemies can use to harm us when we are cradled in your loving care. I know that You are protecting my soldier from those physical enemies he's facing. You are standing guard against the more insidious enemies he's facing, like doubt, fear, and discouragement.

Your presence is with him in a very real way, even as You are with me. Today, no matter what fears come to torment me, I will remember Your promises and stand firm in my faith. Amen

★ ★ ★

*The Lord your God in your midst, The Mighty One, will save; He will rejoice over you with gladness, He will quiet you with His love, He will rejoice over you with singing.*

*Zephaniah 3:17 NKJV*

# MAKE MY SOLDIER'S TRANSITION IN COUNTRY EASY

★ ★ ★

"We aren't just thrown on this earth like dice tossed across a table.
We are lovingly placed here for a purpose."

*Charles R. Swindoll*

*Dear Lord,* I know how hard it can be to get acclimated to another country. Please smooth the transition for my loved one as she gets used to her new environment. Don't let the time change exhaust her and put her in danger.

She'll be traveling there on airplanes, buses, and other modes of transportation. Keep her safe on the way to her destination. Keep any enemies far from her and from those who are traveling with her.

Make the food she has taste good, and don't let the change in her diet upset her system. Don't let the climate be too much of a shock to her system. Give her things that are familiar and remind her of home.

I know she'll be lonely and homesick, but keep her busy and her mind occupied so the time passes quickly. Make sure she gets regular letters and packages from home, so she knows how much we miss her. Keep her safe while she's away and bring her home safe to us. Amen

★ ★ ★

*The Lord will watch over your coming and going both now and forevermore.*

*Psalm 121:8 NIV*

# GUARD MY LOVED ONE'S MIND

★　★　★

*"For happiness one needs security, but joy can spring
like a flower even from the cliffs of despair."*

*Anne Morrow Lindbergh*

*Dear Lord,* I worry about the toll this deployment is taking on my loved one's mind. I'm asking You to guard his mind. Keep him safe from any damage he might have emotionally, psychologically, and spiritually. I hear so much about the trouble our troops have after coming home. Please don't let this happen to my soldier.

I know he's seen things that are horrible, and that scares me. No matter what he sees and/or experiences, let it be balanced with the certain knowledge that there's an ultimate purpose in what he's doing. Show him how You are using these situations for good. Let him have a glimpse of the eternal purpose of what he's experiencing.

Don't let his mind dwell on the what-ifs of the situations surrounding him. Let his mind be at peace and know that You're in control—no matter what happens. I know his heart and how tender it is. Please keep it safe. Amen

★　★　★

*He will call on me, and I will answer him; I will be with him in trouble, I will deliver him and honor him.*

*Psalm 91:15 NIV*

# BRING MY LOVED ONE HOME SAFELY

★ ★ ★

*"Hope is faith holding out its hand in the dark."*

*George Iles*

*Dear Lord,* I know it's time for my loved one to come home from the war. I'm so excited about that, but I'm also scared about her travel. I know she'll have to come home in stages, and I'm worried about her safety as she makes her way home.

Go before her and clear her path of anything that could cause her harm. Make sure the trucks and buses she'll travel on have been thoroughly inspected. Make certain the places she sleeps as she travels are safe from any kind of enemy attack.

Provide qualified people to inspect the airplane before it takes off with her in it, and give her the best pilots to insure her safety while she's in the air. Keep any enemies who want to intercept her from being successful.

Keep the weather calm so it cannot interfere with her travel, and keep the world from any kind of major disaster that would keep her from coming home as soon as possible. I know You're going to be with her wherever and whenever she starts home, and I thank You for watching over her. Amen

★ ★ ★

*But you will not leave in haste or go in flight; for the Lord will go before you, the God of Israel will be your rear guard.*

*Isaiah 52:12 NIV*

# PEACE

Peace can be elusive, even in the ordinary routine of everyday life. Peace in the middle of a war zone is unthinkable—until we turn to God—then it settles joyfully over our minds and heart.

# TEACH MY LOVED ONE TO PRAY

★   ★   ★

"Prayer is not asking. Prayer is putting oneself in
the hands of God, at His disposition, and listening to
His voice in the depth of our hearts."

*Mother Teresa*

*Dear Lord,* just as You've grown my prayer life during my loved one's time away at war, I'm asking You to grow her prayer life. Give her times of prayer with You when the conversation feels so real she looks around to see if You're there in person.

Teach her how to have an ongoing conversation with You and let her learn to recognize Your voice, even if chaos is all around. Make her so tuned in to You she can hear Your tiniest whisper. Then cause her to long to hear more and more from You.

Let her experience all the extremes of prayer—from the joy of instantly answered prayer to the deep abiding sense of satisfaction that comes with waiting to hear from You. Make prayer so second nature to her that no matter what the question, she always turns to You first for the answer.

In everything let my loved one feel Your joy in the time she spends with You. Amen

★   ★   ★

*He was praying in a certain place, and when He finished, one of His disciples said to Him, "Lord, teach us to pray, just as John also taught his disciples."*

*Luke 11:1 HCSB*

# PUT MY SOLDIER'S MIND AT REST

★ ★ ★

"Peace can't be forced, only discovered from within."

*Héctor Martínez*

*Dear Lord,* my prayer today is for my loved one's peace of mind. I'm sitting at home safe, and I'm finding it difficult to have peace. I can't imagine how hard it is for him when he's half a world away and in the midst of a war. But I also know how important it is that he's in good condition physically and mentally. And for that, he needs to have as much peace of mind as possible.

Right now I'm asking You to take away anything that's adding stress in his life. Give him ease in his relationships with those around him, as well as those in command over him and those below him. Remove the small things that can begin as irritations and grow into full-blown anxiety. Give him patience when others irritate him, and grant them the same.

Keep his schedule as regulated as possible. And give him friends that he can relax with. Make sure he has enough time for rest and recreation but not enough time for boredom to set in.

I know You're working in his life, and I thank You for keeping him safe. Please let him see the work You're doing around and through him. Amen

★ ★ ★

*You will keep in perfect peace those whose minds are steadfast, because they trust in You.*

*Isaiah 26:3 NIV*

# COMFORT MY SOLDIER
# WITH YOUR PRESENCE

★ ★ ★

"His center is everywhere; His circumference is nowhere."

*Henry Law*

*Dear Lord,* I know my loved one feels so alone. I want more than anything to be with her, but I know I can't. But You can, and my prayer is for her to feel You constantly by her side. Protect her, guide her, and encourage her with Your presence.

During those times when she's on patrol, give her the insight she needs to stay safe, and keep those around her safe. Help her see any traps the enemy may have set.

Help her know the minds and hearts of those around her so she won't be deceived by a hidden enemy. Give her the insight she needs to get along with her friends and comrades. Don't let any of them be sidetracked by petty quarrels or irritations. They are all under such pressure it's easy for the small things to get blown completely out of perspective.

Use her to bring comfort to those she's serving with. And use others to comfort her. Give her the friends she needs to fight loneliness. Make sure they all stay focused on You and never forget You are always there. Amen

★ ★ ★

*"You will seek Me and find Me when you search for Me with all your heart."*

*Jeremiah 29:13 NASB*

# I'M SO THANKFUL
# FOR YOUR PEACE

★　★　★

"Rest and be thankful."

*William Wordsworth*

*Dear Lord,* I'm so thankful that You are the Prince of Peace. You have shown me that no matter what situation I'm in, all I have to do is turn to You to find peace. Because of this, I can be confident that You are providing that same comfort for my soldier.

Even though his situation is much more extreme, I know You are able to wrap him in that same peace. Your gift is so much deeper than anything we can find in the physical world around us.

Your peace comes in the form of a real person. You are sitting at the right hand of God and, at the same instant, wrapping us in a love so strong that nothing can pull us from Your grasp. Although my soldier and I are separated by miles, we share the same peace.

How can I thank You for this precious gift? When I think of how much You love us, my mind is quiet. The fears I've been battling disappear. I know You are doing the same exact thing for my soldier. Amen

★　★　★

*"These things I have spoken to you, so that in Me you may have peace. In the world you have tribulation, but take courage; I have overcome the world."*

*John 16:33 NASB*

# FINDING PEACE
# IN THE MIDST OF WAR

★ ★ ★

"Like a spring of pure water, God's peace in our hearts brings
cleansing and refreshment to our minds and bodies."

*Billy Graham*

*Dear Lord,* I'm asking You to give my loved one the peace she
needs to get through this deployment. I know she's struggling to
adjust and make sense out of the situations around her. Help her
find Your perspective in all that she's experiencing. Guard her heart
with the perfect peace that can only come from You.

Remind her that You're watching over her, keeping her safe. Let
her see the evidence of Your care every time she goes out. I know
she's not where she is by accident, but this somehow fits into the
plan You have for her life. Show her how You're going to use these
circumstances in her life.

When my loved one runs into things that don't make sense,
hold her close and let her see them through Your eyes. Give her
confirmation of Your constant and abiding love, no matter what's
happening around her. You promise us peace, no matter where we
are. Show her just how powerful You are by providing that peace in
the midst of war. Amen

★ ★ ★

*Now may the Lord of peace Himself give you peace always in every way.
The Lord be with you all.*

*2 Thessalonians 3:16 NKJV*

# GRANT MY SOLDIER AND HIS COMPANIONS A SABBATH REST

★ ★ ★

"As sure as ever God puts His children in the furnace,
He will be in the furnace with them."

*Charles Spurgeon*

*Dear Lord,* You are the God of peace, and I'm praying that You would give my soldier and his companions a peaceful day. I know that they are in the midst of a struggle. Everything about their situation is stressful. Give them a quiet day of rest.

Remove them from the cares and concerns that surround them. Let them hear from You clearly as You speak peace into their weary souls. No matter what their physical location, wrap them in beauty and joy.

Remind them that in You can be found a peace that passes all understanding. Renew their spirit as they drink in Your presence. Give them the camaraderie found in those who call You Lord. In the midst of this war they are surrounded with tragedy and destruction. Replace those images with Your perfect rest.

Refresh and renew each of them as they partake of fellowship with You and with each other. Let them share memories that reinforce who You are and how much You love each of us. Amen

★ ★ ★

*So there is still a Sabbath rest for God's people.*

*Hebrews 4:9 NIRV*

# LET MY LOVED ONE
# SEE BEAUTY EVERY DAY

★  ★  ★

"The earth laughs in flowers."

*Ralph Waldo Emerson*

*Dear Lord,* I know my loved one is in the midst of an ugly situation, but I'm asking You to give her glimpses of beauty every day she's there. I know there must be some beauty around her. It could be the sweetness of someone doing something for someone else or a small flower that's managed to survive and flourish in spite of the war.

Teach her to recognize beauty when it appears. Then make sure she shares it with those nearby, so they can all take comfort in it.

Let her be an example of the good that's happening over there. Use her skills to protect those who cannot protect themselves. Make sure she's aware of how You are using her to reach out to others and bring something lovely to their lives.

Most of all, never let her doubt that there's a purpose to Your plan for her circumstances. Make sure she knows how much we all value her sacrifice and are proud of her willingness to serve others. Amen

★  ★  ★

*He has made everything beautiful in its time. Also He has put eternity in their hearts, except that no one can find out the work that God does from beginning to end.*

*Ecclesiastes 3:11 NKJV*

# REASSURE MY SOLDIER

★　★　★

"Cleverness is cheap. It is faith that He praises."

*George MacDonald*

*Dear Lord,* I know that at times my soldier must feel like he's caught in a nightmare. He must feel trapped by circumstances that are beyond his control. Please show him that these circumstances are not beyond Your control.

How hard it is to understand these times. There seem to be wars everywhere we look. I know he's tired of the fight, but stand with him, and give him hope. Help him to look to You before his burdens become too much to bear. My heart is torn to pieces thinking of what he's being called to do.

Show him how these circumstances work for good in the world. Give him the ability to see the good things that I know are happening all around him. You can be there when I can't. Reassure him that You're all he needs, no matter what happens. Amen

★　★　★

*Therefore, my dear brothers, be steadfast, immovable, always excelling in the Lord's work, knowing that your labor in the Lord is not in vain.*

*1 Corinthians 15:58 HCSB*

# KEEP MY LOVED ONE FROM WORRY ABOUT HER CHILDREN

★ ★ ★

"Our victory rests not on faith in our spirituality.
Our victory rests on faith in our God."

*Beth Moore*

*Dear Lord,* as my loved one serves in the military half a world away, I pray she wouldn't have any reasons to worry about her children. Give her a perfect peace about how healthy and well cared for they are while she's gone. Don't let her mind be sidetracked with worry about how they are acting or even how fearful for her they are.

Let her hear from others how well they're doing, even though they miss her more than anything. Give her packages and letters from home, filled with their pictures and things they've made just for her.

Reassure her they are coping well and that others back home are filling in until she can be reunited with them. Keep her from feeling like she's being replaced by those who are just helping. Remind her that as much as she loves her kids, You love all of us even more. Amen

★ ★ ★

*Can any one of you by worrying add a single hour to your life?*

*Matthew 6:27 NIV*

# THANK YOU FOR
# THE PEACE YOU PROVIDE

★　★　★

"When it is dark enough, you can see the stars."
*Ralph Waldo Emerson*

*Dear Lord,* praying for peace when my loved one is in the midst of war seems an impossible request. But I have experienced that peace and know that with You all things are possible. Your peace isn't found in a cessation of war. It's found in a person. When we know Your Son, we know the Author of peace.

You have provided a victorious way for us to face whatever this world holds. As we take hold of that peace, it becomes a beacon, calling everyone who can see it to join us. What a great blessing to be Your child.

The world would have us believe that peace isn't possible in a world at war. But I know differently. I am Your child, and I have the confidence and underlying joy that comes from knowing I am loved. Remind my soldier of these things. Surround him with people who exhibit this peace.

Peace in the time of war isn't just a dream; when we come to You, it becomes the reality that undergirds our lives. We are so blessed to call You Father and to have Your protection surround us, no matter where we are. Amen

★　★　★

*The Lord gives His people strength; the Lord blesses His people with peace.*

*Psalm 29:11 HCSB*

# GRANT MY SOLDIER PEACE WHEN SHE'S EXHAUSTED

★ ★ ★

*"Peace with God is where all peace begins."*

*Jim Gallery*

*Dear Lord,* I sense that my loved one is struggling right now. She's so tired, and beyond that, she's dealing with extremes I can't imagine. One minute she's in the midst of chaos and terror and the next trying to cope with boredom. The extremes are wearing her down. Help her rely on You as life reels out of control. Be her firm foundation.

I know that just like her circumstances go from one extreme to another, so do her emotions. She's experiencing them all, from joy to terror and everything in between. She needs Your support now more than ever before.

Protect her from exhaustion, and the despair that often comes with it. Give her time to rest physically. Put people around who can help her process the emotions she's feeling and seeing in others.

Most of all let her feel Your presence as You give her a sense of peace that is totally at odds with her surroundings. Wrap her in Your love, giving her proof that You will never leave or abandon her. Let my loved one see You at work in the chaos and catch glimpses of Your protection. Amen

★ ★ ★

*Cast all your anxiety on him because he cares for you.*

*1 Peter 5:7 NIV*

# DON'T EVER LET THE LONELINESS BECOME TOO MUCH

★   ★   ★

"We need never shout across the spaces to an absent God.
He is nearer than our own soul,
closer than our most secret thoughts."

*A. W. Tozer*

*Dear Lord,* I know how much I miss my loved one, and I'm surrounded by the familiarity of home. I can't imagine how lonely he is. Comfort him with Your presence, and remind him that You will never abandon him.

I'm afraid he feels like the rest of the world is moving forward and he's stuck in one place. Give him the proof he needs that he has not been forgotten by those at home. Overwhelm him with letters and packages. Don't let a single mail call pass without a reminder of how much we love him.

I'm so proud of him and his willingness to sacrifice. Let him see the impact his service has in the world today, as well as the future and even into eternity.

When he aches to feel a hug from home, replace that longing with the warmth of Your love. Make it so real that he'll have no doubt You're there with him. Don't ever let him feel abandoned by me or anyone else he loves. Amen

★   ★   ★

*All my longings lie open before you, Lord; my sighing is not hidden from you.*

*Psalm 38:9 NIV*

# GIVE MY SOLDIER
# A LIKE-MINDED COMPANION

★　★　★

"No one can take the place of a friend, no one."
*Maya Angelou*

*Dear Lord,* You have provided so many people to come alongside me and help me cope. I'm praying for You to provide a like-minded companion for my soldier. She's in a strange land, surrounded by dangers I don't even want to imagine. Give her a friend who shares her faith to come alongside during this time.

Give her someone who understands her and values the same things she does. Let her have a friend who laughs at the same things and will talk or listen when my soldier needs to be heard.

Wrap my loved one up in Your tender care. Make sure she sees Your presence in the friends who surround her. Guard her from behind and ahead. Go before her when she leaves the base on patrol and when she returns tired beyond belief.

When fear comes in waves, give her someone to share it with. Calm her anxious thoughts and her mind by providing her a trust-worthy confidante. Reassure her of Your presence through her friend in times of quiet and times of chaos.

Let them reinforce the foundation of faith they share, and guard them from all who would try to destroy it. Amen

★　★　★

*Whatever you have learned or received or heard from me, or seen in me—put it into practice. And the God of peace will be with you.*

*Philippians 4:9 NIV*

# COMFORT MY SOLDIER
# SO HE CAN COMFORT OTHERS

★ ★ ★

"When you cannot stand, He will bear you in His arms."

*Francis de Sales*

*Dear Lord,* I know it's hard to be in a strange place with nothing familiar anywhere in sight. This is where my soldier is right now, and I believe he's battling against intense loneliness. Help him conquer these feelings and overcome the sadness he feels.

I know he's not the only one over there who's lonely. Help him find others to share these feelings. Let them become a source of comfort and peace for each other. Grow their friendship into something strong that can support them when they're struggling.

Bring memories to mind that bring him comfort, but don't let him be overwhelmed with loneliness by dwelling on what he's missing. Comfort him with how much we miss him, and how proud we are of the job he's doing and the sacrifice he's chosen to make.

Remind him that he will have good times when he returns. Make the time pass swiftly for us all and reunite us soon as a family. Amen

★ ★ ★

*Even though I walk through the valley of the shadow of death, I fear no evil, for You are with me; Your rod and Your staff, they comfort me.*

*Psalm 23:4 NASB*

# WITH YOU I KNOW WE HAVE NOTHING TO FEAR

★ ★ ★

*"Be assured, if you walk with Him and look to Him,*
*and expect help from Him, He will never fail you."*

*George Mueller*

*Dear Lord,* this is such a difficult time. I hate being separated from my loved one. I hate that she's having to go through the things she's facing. But no matter what is happening with either of us, with You by our side, I know we have nothing to fear.

You are our defender, able to protect us from any enemy. You are everywhere, in every time. There is no trap or ambush available to those who would attack Your children. You even protect us from ourselves.

As my soldier is fighting half a world away, I know there is no reason to fear. I can have confidence in Your ability to defend her and keep her safe. There is nothing on heaven or on earth that can defeat You.

I pray that You will remind my loved one of this. Make sure she knows that You are always there with her and that she has nothing to fear. Show her Your provision and care You take to keep her safe, no matter what is going on around her. Amen

★ ★ ★

*So we say with confidence, "The Lord is my helper; I will not be afraid.*
*What can mere mortals do to me?"*

*Hebrews 13:6 NIV*

# PROTECT MY LOVED ONE FROM BEING DISCOURAGED

★  ★  ★

"We must accept finite disappointment,
but never lose infinite hope."

*Martin Luther King, Jr.*

*Dear Lord,* please keep my loved one from getting discouraged while he's deployed. He's away for so long, I know it's hard. Everything around him is strange and unfamiliar.

He's got to feel like his life has turned into a nightmare that's never going to end. Please protect him from feelings of despair. It would be so easy for him to give in, but I know he can stay strong. I'm asking You to help him.

Give him friends who understand what he's feeling, and bind them together into a group that provides the encouragement they each need. Let him have a chance to spend time in normal pursuits, watching a movie, reading, or just hanging out with his buddies.

Here at home bring him to the minds of his friends and family so they can keep him in their constant prayers. Don't let him feel abandoned or like the world has forgotten him. Let him know that it not only means so much to us, but that his willingness to do the hard things has eternal significance and is making a real difference in the world around him. Amen

★  ★  ★

*Taste and see that the Lord is good; blessed is the one who takes refuge in him.*

*Psalm 34:8 NIV*

# GIVE MY LOVED ONE
# A WORD FROM HOME

★ ★ ★

"Memories are the stars that brighten our dreams."

*Sharon Repp*

*Dear Lord,* my loved one is far from home, and I know she's lonely for the things that are familiar and dear to her heart. I'm asking You to give her something from home to comfort her. Let her have the chance to make a call or connect with those she loves and who love her so much.

Let today be the day she receives a box from home or even sees a familiar face she didn't expect. Give her a taste or a smell that takes her back to the places she loves so much. And let that touch fill her with hope and not despair.

I worry about her state of mind when she's lonely. Please keep up her spirits. Give her friends to help, as well as buddies she can help and encourage. Bring memories to her mind that fill her with joy and laughter. Let her remember the fun times, the silly times, even the crazy things she did when she was young. Give her the opportunity to share those memories so that she and her friends can be encouraged. Most of all, be there with her, no matter what. Amen

★ ★ ★

*May the God of hope fill you with all joy and peace as you trust in him, so that you may overflow with hope by the power of the Holy Spirit.*

*Romans 15:13 NIV*

# PROTECT MY LOVED ONE FROM DESPAIR

★ ★ ★

"It is impossible for that man to despair
who remembers that his Helper is omnipotent."

*Jeremy Taylor*

*Dear Lord,* I know my loved one is going through so much. It's hard for me to understand what he's experiencing. Sometimes when I talk to him, he sounds so discouraged. Protect him from the despair that I know has to be hovering close by him.

Don't let the things he's seeing during this war overcome the good he's experienced in times past. He's always had faith, and I'm asking You to strengthen his faith. Protect him from turning away from You in despair. Don't let him begin to doubt what he knows to be true.

I know You hurt when we hurt. Stand with him now as he grieves for the tragedy around him. Let him see the sorrow in Your heart for what man has inflicted on man. This world isn't what You would have chosen for us, but we overruled Your choice. Remind him that You will one day return everything to the way it was meant to be. Until then, walk with him, comfort him, and surround him with Your love. Amen

★ ★ ★

*We are pressured in everyway but not crushed; we are perplexed but not in despair.*

*2 Corinthians 4:8 HCSB*

# THOSE CLOSE TO MY LOVED ONE

We are rarely alone, and that's the case with those who are on deployment in a war zone. Praying for the people close to our loved ones can have a huge impact on all our lives.

# GIVE MY LOVED ONE STRONG FRIENDSHIPS

★  ★  ★

"There can be no friendship without confidence,
and no confidence without integrity."

*Samuel Johnson*

*Dear Lord,* I'm asking You to surround my loved one with men of faith who will encourage him. As he goes through these difficult circumstances he needs others around him to help him stay strong. He also needs a group where he can be that example of strength for others.

Provide him with strong friendships that help him grow in his knowledge of You. Don't let him get stuck in a group where no one else believes as he does. Guard him from those who would tear down his faith and fill him with doubt.

I pray for those who are his closest friends, and I ask You to keep them from doubts about Your love and faithfulness. Bind a group of them together with love for You. Then give them the courage to share their own fears and worries. Help them grow strong by holding each other accountable and time they need to pray together.

Also give them the opportunity to reach out to others, and bring them into a friendship that shows Your love. Most of all keep them safe and guard them in all ways. Amen

★  ★  ★

*Two are better than one because they have a good return for their labor.*

*Ecclesiastes 4:9 NASB*

# GIVE MY SOLDIER COMMANDERS OF CHARACTER

★ ★ ★

"Leadership is a potent combination of strategy and character.
But if you must be without one, be without strategy."

*Norman Schwarzkopf*

*Dear Lord,* I pray for those in charge of my loved one, for those determining her assignments. Give them wisdom beyond their own earthly abilities. Let them anticipate the actions of the enemy and work to keep their troops from all harm.

Let my loved one be inspired by the wisdom of her commanders. Give her reason to trust them and obey them when the decisions are difficult. Give her commanders the ability to make hard decisions and the patience to keep from acting without thought.

Make her leaders wise in the way of the enemy, as well as in the needs of the troops below them. Give them insight into when to act and when to allow rest. Put men and women of justice over my soldier, and let her see that justice exercised regularly.

Give the commanders Your wisdom and the courage to stand by that wisdom. Let them lead with their hearts, not just their minds. Protect them all and bring them safely home. Amen

★ ★ ★

*To God belong wisdom and power; counsel and understanding are his.*

*Job 12:13 NIV*

# GIVE MY SOLDIER'S COMMANDERS WISDOM

★ ★ ★

"Take time to deliberate; but when the time
for action arrives, stop thinking and go in."

*Andrew Jackson*

*Dear Lord,* bless those who are in command over my soldier. Give them the wisdom they need to keep him safe, as well as the men and women serving with him.

Make them aware of the needs of those serving under them. Even in their strength, give them hearts of compassion. Don't allow them to become hardened to the suffering of others. Never let the lives of those around them be reduced to just numbers.

I'm praying for them to feel Your peace as they make the hard decisions. I can't imagine how difficult it would be to know the lives of others rest in a decision I had to make. Increase their courage, but don't let them become foolhardy.

Protect them from their enemies, and protect their families at home. Keep them from regret and from the despair of second-guessing the decisions they've made. Most of all give them hearts focused on You. Amen

★ ★ ★

*Remember your leaders, who spoke the word of God to you. Consider the outcome of their way of life and imitate their faith.*

*Hebrews 13:7 NIV*

# YOU ARE ALWAYS WITH US

★ ★ ★

"I must first have the sense of God's possession of me
before I can have the sense of His presence with me."

*Watchman Nee*

*Dear Lord,* thank You that You are always with us. You are never
called away from our side by something more important. You have
promised to walk with us, and Your faithfulness knows no bounds.

It's easy to become overwhelmed by the emotions I feel. I'm
thankful that I don't have to rely on how I feel. Anytime I feel dis-
tant, all I have to do is open up the Bible and be reminded how close
You really are. While I sleep, You are there, guarding my dreams and
preventing the fears I feel from turning into nightmares. You will
never leave me or forsake me.

I know that this is true for my soldier as well. You will never
abandon her. I can't imagine what life would be like if I didn't have
Your constant presence to guide and protect me. I'm thankful I
don't ever have to experience that type of existence. Thank You for
sticking with me and never abandoning me. Amen

★ ★ ★

*The Lord is good, a stronghold in the day of trouble, and He knows those
who take refuge in Him.*

*Nahum 1:7 NASB*

# PROTECT MY SOLDIER'S SPOUSE

★ ★ ★

"There is no exercise better for the heart than
reaching down and lifting people up."

*John Holmes*

*Dear Lord,* my focus right now is on my soldier's family as he's away at war. I'm especially praying for his wife. I know how hard it is to have someone You love in harm's way; it must be even more difficult to have a spouse in danger. I'm asking You to protect her. While my loved one is away, be the provider and support she needs.

When she's lonely give her the comfort she needs. Let her hear from him regularly, and don't let me neglect her in any way when I can help ease her burden. Don't let her friends forget to include her, even though her spouse is away. Keep her so busy with invitations and encouragement that she welcomes time alone.

Give him the ability to talk to his wife regularly. Guard their marriage during this separation, and make sure they grow closer together instead of farther apart. Keep them both from any kind of temptation that could insert itself into their relationship. Look after her and protect her while her husband is away. Be everything she needs and most of all, help the time they are apart pass quickly. Amen

★ ★ ★

*"What therefore God has joined together, let no man separate."*

*Mark 10:9 NASB*

# SURROUND MY LOVED ONE
# WITH A GROUP OF BELIEVERS

★ ★ ★

"No friendship is an accident."

*O. Henry*

*Dear Lord,* while my loved one is away at war I'm praying for You to create a small pocket of Your kingdom right where she is. Give her the same resources there that she has here. Make sure she has access to someone who can give her spiritual guidance and speak Your truth.

Provide the friendship she needs with others who have the same values and beliefs that she's grown up with. Help them find regular times to meet together for worship and prayer. Keep others from ridiculing them or harassing them because of their faith. Instead let them be an example of how Your kingdom here on earth really works.

In the midst of this, give my loved one the accountability she needs with a few close friends. Let them build a trust in each other so they know they can share their struggles.

I pray that no one in her chain of command will permit any roadblocks as she exercises her beliefs. Go before her and clear the way. Build the foundation she needs for this sanctuary. Amen

★ ★ ★

*[Do] not giving up meeting together, as some are in the habit of doing, but encouraging one another—and all the more as you see the Day approaching.*

*Hebrews 10:25 NIV*

# PROTECT OUR MARRIAGE

★ ★ ★

"A successful marriage requires falling in love many times,
always with the same person."

*Mignon McLaughlin*

*Dear Lord,* please protect our marriage while my spouse is deployed. It's so hard being married while he's serving. Help us both stay focused on keeping our relationship healthy.

Surround him with friends who value his commitment and won't lead him astray. Give him things to help keep busy so he won't be tempted by boredom. Use this time apart to bring us closer together and remind us why we love each other.

I know he wants to protect me, and keep me from worrying, but don't let him bottle up his feelings and try to protect me. Give him the courage to share his struggles with me. Show him that by being honest we'll grow closer together instead of farther apart.

As this time apart goes by, don't let him give up on our marriage. Show him it's worth the effort and worth the loneliness. Give me ways to assure him of my feelings so he can continue to be confident of my loyalty and love. Amen

★ ★ ★

*That is why a man leaves his father and mother and is united to his wife, and they become one flesh.*

*Genesis 2:24 NIV*

# DON'T LET MY SOLDIER WORRY ABOUT THOSE AT HOME

★ ★ ★

"Do not anticipate trouble, or worry about
what may never happen. Keep in the sunlight."

*Benjamin Franklin*

*Dear Lord,* don't let my loved one worry about us here at home. I know she feels torn between the duty she's committed to and taking care of us. Give her the assurance she needs to focus wholly on the job she has to do. Keep her worry free when it comes to her family and those at home.

Even though she's confident that we're okay, I know worry can still creep in. Make sure the packages and letters we send arrive exactly when she needs them. Don't let there be delays that cause her to become anxious about how we're coping. Give her evidence of how our friends are rallying around and taking up the slack while she's away serving.

As others step in to help, don't ever let her feel she's been replaced. Balance her assurance about how well we're doing with the certain knowledge that it's never as good as when she's around. Amen

★ ★ ★

*Anxiety in a man's heart weighs it down, but a good word makes it glad.*

*Proverbs 12:25 NASB*

# CARE FOR MY LOVED ONE'S CHILDREN

★ ★ ★

"Home is the nicest word there is."

*Laura Ingalls Wilder*

*Dear Lord,* protect my loved one's children while he's away at war. I know they struggle to understand why he has to go, even while they are proud of his sacrifice. It's so hard for them to be without him.

I pray that their friends will show them the support and patience they need. I ask that their teachers will understand how this situation may affect their behavior.

Keep them from acting out with negative behaviors when they struggle, but instead lead them to share what they're feeling to those who can help. Also make the adults in their lives more aware of what these children who are missing their dads are feeling.

Make sure they get the chance to talk to their dad regularly. Help them not to be angry because he's gone or resent him for leaving to fight in this war. Give their mother the extra patience she needs, and cause my loved one's children to work with her, not against her while she's gone.

They are so young, so please be the stable foundation they need while she's away. Keep them safe and keep them from fear. Amen

★ ★ ★

*And he took the children in his arms, placed his hands on them and blessed them.*

*Mark 10:16 NIV*

# BLESS THE FRIENDS
# MY LOVED ONE LEFT BEHIND

★  ★  ★

"However rare true love may be, it is less so than true friendship."
*Albert Einstein*

*Dear Lord,* while my loved one is at war, I'm praying for the close friends she's left behind. I know they worry about her and want to reach out and help, but many aren't exactly sure how to do that. Give them the knowledge they need to be able to support her while she's away.

Don't let them forget about her while she's away. Bring her to their minds frequently so they will continually pray for her. Encourage them to send her letters and emails from home. Don't let them keep their own day-to-day happenings from her because they're afraid it will make her feel worse. Instead help them share all the small things that give her a feeling of being connected to a world she holds dear.

Keep her friends safe while she's away. Help them make good decisions and stay focused on the things that are good for their lives, and especially keep them from physical harm. Keep them safe in mind, body, and soul. Amen

★  ★  ★

*Therefore comfort one another with these words.*

*1 Thessalonians 4:18 NASB*

# HELP MY SOLDIER BE A FRIEND TO THOSE IN NEED

★   ★   ★

"A true friend unbosoms freely, advises justly, assists readily, adventures boldly, takes all patiently, defends courageously, and continues a friend unchangeably."

*William Penn*

*Dear Lord,* I'm praying for my loved one to be a strong friend to those around him. You've put him in the middle of a lot of lonely people. Give him a heart to see those around him who are hurting and need the encouragement of a true friend. I am asking you to provide friends to fill the empty hours ahead of him.

Let them form a small pocket of Your kingdom and protect them from those who would seek to tear them apart. Help them encourage each other and hold each other accountable. Use him to reinforce wise decisions of his friends. Give them the type of friendship where they can hold each other accountable when any of them would deviate from doing what's right.

Show them what it means to have a friend and be a friend. Teach them the joy of friendship and the freedom found in a group that is trustworthy. Amen

★   ★   ★

*He who walks with wise men will be wise, but the companion of fools will suffer harm.*

*Proverbs 13:20 NASB*

# KEEP MY SOLDIER'S FRIENDS AT HOME SAFE

★ ★ ★

"It is only the fear of God that can deliver us
from the fear of man."

*John Witherspoon*

*Dear Lord,* I know my loved one misses her family, but she also misses her friends. She's got some new friends with her now, but those she's left behind are still important to her. I'm praying for them today. I know they worry about her so much.

Comfort them, Lord. Give them Your strength to endure this time spent apart. Make sure they don't hide what they're feeling, but let her know how much she's missed.

I know they're concerned about her safety, just like the rest of us. Give them plenty of opportunities to hear from her. Use this time to grow their faith in You, and teach them how trustworthy You are. Let my loved one's faith and strength be an inspiration.

Keep her friends safe, too, while she's away. Don't let anything happen to them. Guard their families and keep them all safe, physically, emotionally, and spiritually. Amen

★ ★ ★

*An enemy might defeat one person, but two people together can defend themselves; a rope that is woven of three strings is hard to break.*

*Ecclesiastes 4:12 NCV*

# RELIEVE MY LOVED ONE OF FINANCIAL WORRIES BACK HOME

★ ★ ★

"Worry divides the mind."

*Max Lucado*

*Dear Lord,* I know my loved one is worried about his family, especially about their money situation. He knows they're struggling to stay afloat financially. This adds so much to his stress and to the burden he's already carrying.

Provide for his family in such a visible and abundant way that he won't have to worry. Give him the proof he needs to see You at work at home. Put people around his family to help when they need it. Keep them focused on reducing his stress instead of not imposing on friends and family.

Show him, by providing for his family, how much You honor his sacrifice and his obedience. He's chosen to do the hard things in life and follow You no matter what. Give him the assurance that he's made the right choice.

Use this difficult time financially to grow his faith and show him exactly what it means to rely on You in every circumstance. Keep us all humble, and don't let us believe our success rests in us but only in You. Amen

★ ★ ★

*Every good gift and every perfect gift is from above, and comes down from the Father of lights, with whom there is no variation or shadow of turning.*

*James 1:17 NKJV*

# GRANT MY SOLDIER UNITY WITH HER COMRADES

★  ★  ★

"Actions, not words, are the true criterion
of the attachment of friends."

*George Washington*

*Dear Lord,* I know my loved one has trained for the mission she's on. And I also know she and those she's serving with have been together long enough to build trust and camaraderie. As they face this deployment and move into a battle zone, allow nothing to disrupt their unity.

Give them minds and hearts that are set on the same goals and objectives. Don't let lack of sleep or any other disruptions cause minor conflicts. Be there with my loved one and those she's deployed with, and constantly keep watch on their minds and hearts.

Protect them from anyone who would purposely disrupt their unity. Give them insight into the motivations behind any disruptions. Make them quick to forgive those whose outbursts are unintentional and quick to call out those who seek only to destroy.

Make them transparent to each other, and build their trust to such a level that they don't even have to doubt what's happening when one of them stumbles. Increase their level of accountability with one another, and most of all never let them forget that You are with them. Amen

★  ★  ★

*Above all, put on love—the perfect bond of unity.*

*Colossians 3:14 HCSB*

129

# GIVE MY SOLDIER FREEDOM TO WORSHIP YOU

★　★　★

"You may go through difficulty, hardship, or trial—but as long as you are anchored to Him, you will have hope."

*Charles Stanley*

*Dear Lord,* the political climate that surrounds us right now is frightening. It feels like everything we believe in is under attack. I know that it's becoming more and more difficult for my loved one to feel comfortable as a believer in today's military. Protect him from all those who would restrict his freedom to worship.

Give him the strength to stand up to those who would limit his worship and Bible study time. Don't let those around him stop him from sharing Your great love and peace. Don't let him be passed up for promotion because he chooses to make his love for You a public part of who he is.

Soften the hearts of those who would deny Your sovereignty and love. Give him opportunities to speak Your truth without censorship. But no matter what, give him the strength to never compromise as he serves You with an undivided heart.

Put him in the midst of like-minded companions who are bold. Don't let his boldness become arrogance, but keep it seasoned with humility and exercised in love. Amen

★　★　★

*And now, Lord, listen to their threats. Lord, help us, your servants, to speak your word without fear.*

*Acts 4:29 NCV*

# GUARD MY SOLDIER'S MARRIAGE

★ ★ ★

"The pain of parting is nothing to the joy of meeting again."

*Charles Dickens*

*Dear Lord,* keep my loved one from worry while she's deployed. I know her thoughts are on her family, and she wants them to be safe. Even more, she wants to be with them, keeping them safe. But she has a job to do, and while she's making this sacrifice, give her the peace of mind she needs to stay focused.

I know how precious her family is. Guard her marriage while she's away. Make sure she and her spouse are kept far from any temptation that could hurt them. Let her see how those back home are stepping in and serving her spouse while she's away. Remove all the worry she has about financial matters, and replace that with thankfulness as she sees her family embraced and cared for by her community.

Let her have regular opportunities to speak to her spouse, through the Internet and the telephone. Make their conversations sweet, as they stumble over each other's words in their excitement to share what is most important. Don't let awkward pauses or misunderstandings take away the joy of their brief times together.

Deepen their love for each other, and grow their relationship with You. Teach them to rely on You. Amen

★ ★ ★

*For this reason a man will leave his father and mother and be united to his wife.*

*Mark 10:7 NIV*

# THANK YOU FOR
# MY LOVED ONE'S FAMILY

★  ★  ★

"Our 'safe place' is not where we live; it is in whom we live."

*Tom White*

*Dear Lord,* thank You for providing my soldier with such a loving family. They support him and his decision to serve in so many ways. I know my loved one worries about his family when he's so far away. But he also can have confidence that they understand why he's chosen this path.

Instead of berating him for his decision, I see how they work together, learning and growing through the difficult times. Remind him that You, God, are the Father to the fatherless. Show him how You're growing their faith through this hard time.

I love how they each find special ways to let him know how much they miss him. But with the hardships come the sweet successes. While he's far away, let him see the good that's coming out of the separation, even though it's a painful time them all.

Most of all, give him plenty of opportunities to communicate with the kids, through phone calls, over the Internet, and with packages. Show him how proud they are of their father and how much they respect the job he's doing and the sacrifice he's chosen to make. Amen

★  ★  ★

*Children are a heritage from the Lord, offspring a reward from him.*

*Psalm 127:3 NIV*

# USE THE FRIENDS OF MY LOVED ONE TO ENCOURAGE HER

★　★　★

"Words are easy, like the wind; faithful friends are hard to find."

*William Shakespeare*

*Dear Lord,* I want to thank You for the companions You've put in my loved one's life. I know she has friends to help watch her back in battle, as well as when she's at rest. I'm praying for these comrades. I'm asking You to watch over them and protect them, even as You're looking out for my loved one.

Continue to strengthen their bonds of friendship. Give them opportunities to laugh and have fun together, always encouraging each other. Most of all help them grow in their love and service for You. Let them see You at work around them and through them.

Use their friendship to spur each other on to great things. Guard them from any negative talk or behavior. Give them wisdom to make right decisions and guard themselves from actions they'll later regret.

I know they all have families back home. They have parents, spouses, and even children who are as worried about their loved ones as I am about my soldier. Give their families regular contact with those who are at war, so they know the one they love is safe. Comfort these families, even as You comfort me. Amen

★　★　★

*As iron sharpens iron, so a man sharpens the countenance of his friend.*

*Proverbs 27:17 NKJV*

# PRAYERS
# FOR ME

# FEAR

Sometimes it's impossible to pray for someone when we're overwhelmed with terror. When we connect with God, He will calm our fears and give us the strength we need.

# STAYING STRONG

"The only way to learn strong faith is to endure great trials."

*Charles Mueller*

★   ★   ★

*Dear Lord,* help me feel Your presence as I struggle to stay strong while my loved one is away at war. At times I feel so alone and without hope. I know that's not true, that You are always with me, but sometimes the fear overwhelms me and drives out everything else.

I need to find a way to stay focused on You, no matter what I'm feeling. It's so hard because the fear can paralyze me and keep me from doing the things I should to get back on track. I'm asking for Your help with this. Give me some concrete things I can do to combat this.

I feel like such a failure and like I've let down everyone, especially my loved one. I want to be strong for her, so she can be proud of me. Instead I'm weak and unable to even control my own thoughts. Help me with this.

Bring someone into my life who has struggled with this and been able to overcome it. I need to see that a victory is possible, and then I need help to make it happen in my life. Amen

★   ★   ★

*I will not fear though tens of thousands assail me on every side.*

*Psalm 3:6 NIV*

# THE DARK PIT OF FEAR

"A string of opinions no more constitutes faith,
than a string of beads constitutes holiness."

*John Wesley*

★   ★   ★

*Dear Lord,* once more I find myself in that dark pit of fear. Every time I shut my eyes I see images of my loved one wounded or worse. I have to have sleep, but the nights are punctuated with nightmares. Help me, Lord. Protect me from these things that leave me weak with fright.

Reassure me that You are still in control. Give me the assurance I need to believe You are at work protecting my soldier. I know the danger he's in. Even though I try not to think about it, the news reports it every time I walk by a television. How do I insulate myself from the terrible knowledge of what he's facing?

I cringe as I think about what could happen. I don't know how to turn off my mind. Help me!

I know my only hope is in You. You will have to be my shield as I try to cope with the dangers surrounding my loved one. The Bible promises that You are all powerful, and I'm begging You to protect him. Keep him safe as he serves, and give me the assurance I need to cope while he's away. Amen

★   ★   ★

*The Lord is my light and my salvation—whom should I fear? The Lord is the stronghold of my life—of whom should I be afraid?*

*Psalm 27:1 HCSB*

# GIVE ME REST FROM MY FEARS

★　★　★

"In the center of a hurricane there is absolute peace and quiet.
There is no safer place than in the center of the will of God."

*Corrie ten Boom*

*Dear Lord,* I'm so exhausted from sleepless nights spent worrying about my loved one. Bad dreams fill my nights, and thoughts of disaster crowd my thoughts each day. My emotions are so sharp and ragged they are cutting my heart to pieces.

Please, God, intervene and give me the rest I need from my fears. Help me believe that You are taking care of the one I love so dearly. You promise to protect us, and I want to have confidence in that, but I'm so scared.

I'm even afraid to ask for proof that You're trustworthy. I don't want to jeopardize my loved one's safety by making You angry. Just giving voice to these thoughts is so hard. You are loving and full of mercy. Forgive me for feeling this way.

You are my strength, and I'm choosing right now to trust You with my loved one. Guard my mind and thoughts from the fear that threatens me on all sides. Be my protector, and, most of all, take care of the one I love. Amen

★　★　★

*There is no fear in love. But perfect love drives out fear, because fear has
to do with punishment. The one who fears is not made perfect in love.*

*1 John 4:18 NIV*

# THANK YOU THAT YOU ARE A GOD WHO NEVER RESTS

★　★　★

"We can be tired, weary and emotionally distraught,
but after spending time alone with God, we find that
He injects into our bodies energy, power and strength."

*Charles Stanley*

*Dear Lord,* You are always with us, even before we cry out. You are a God who never rests. You are always on guard. No matter what we're facing we can be at peace with You near.

Even now I can picture You watching my soldier as he sleeps. You stand guard as he slumbers, protecting him from physical attack as well as from the nightmares that often populate his dreams. With You always on guard, he can get the rest he needs.

When he's out on patrol, You are there with him. You know every hidden bomb and planned attack. Nothing the enemy plans will ever catch You off guard.

No matter what my loved one faces, I can be confident You are there first. Whispering wisdom into his ear. You give his commanders the insight they need to plan the battles and expose the plans of the enemy.

Your heart is set with an inconceivable love for Your children. No one will ever snatch them from your hand. Amen

★　★　★

*He will not allow your foot to slip; He who keeps you will not slumber.*

*Psalm 121:3 NASB*

# LATE-NIGHT BURDENS

★ ★ ★

"God never gives strength for tomorrow, or for the next hour,
but only for the strain of the minute."

*Oswald Chambers*

*Dear Lord,* tonight I'm awake and just can't get my loved one off my mind. My fear for her is a burden my heart just doesn't know how to bear. My mind keeps imagining such horrible scenes of her injured or worse. I need You Lord, and she needs You.

Asking You to keep her safe just doesn't seem powerful enough. But it's all I seem to be able to do. I'm not eloquent, and I don't know the Bible well enough to even know how to pray, but I'm begging You right now to show up where she is and wrap Your protection around her. Call in scores of angels, or whatever it takes to make sure she's okay.

I can't seem to sense whether You hear me or not, so I'm asking You to also give me something so I know You're here, as well as there. I know Your Word promises that You hear when I pray, but I'm just asking for something to help my faith along.

I know in the Bible You showed up in amazing ways and did miraculous things. Do You still work miracles today? Tonight I'm choosing to believe that You do. I'm putting my faith in You. Amen

★ ★ ★

*And not only that, but we also rejoice in our afflictions, because we know that affliction produces endurance, endurance produces proven character, and proven character produces hope.*

*Romans 5:3-4 HCSB*

# BRING MY LOVED ONE
# HOME SAFE

★ ★ ★

"Worry is the senseless process of cluttering up tomorrows opportunities with leftover problems from today."

*Barbara Johnson*

*Dear Lord,* this loved one of mine is infinitely precious to me. I can't imagine life without him, and it scares me so much to think about what the future may hold. I want to be seen as brave, but I don't really want to be that person. All I want is the one I love back with me, safe and whole.

Help me navigate this time away from him. The separation is bad enough, but to add the danger I know he's facing on a daily basis makes this almost unbearable. I just want it to be over.

I want to help him stay safe. I want to pray powerful prayers that will sway You to keep him in Your protection, but I know that's not how it works. I'm powerless in this situation, but I know You are all powerful. And it's that power I'm asking You to bring to bear on his behalf.

The Bible tells me You love each of us even more than we can love each other. So I'm turning him over to You. Shield him from all harm, physical, mental, and emotional and bring him home safe to me. Amen

★ ★ ★

*Surely, Lord, You bless the righteous; You surround them with Your favor as with a shield.*

*Psalm 5:12 NIV*

# PEACE

Finding peace when someone we love is in danger is an almost impossible task—until we turn the problem over to God. He will step in with a peace that defies description!

# YOUR PERFECT PEACE

★ ★ ★

"Worrying does not empty tomorrow of its troubles,
it empties today of its strength."

*Corrie ten Boom*

*Dear Lord,* as I sit here, drowning in worry about how my loved one is doing, give me peace. Teach me how to move beyond the fear, even if it never goes completely away. Use this time to grow my faith and to make me into someone who takes everything to You in prayer.

Give me the assurance I need to know You are hearing my heartfelt cries for my loved one's safety. Even when the words won't come, allow me to feel the peace of knowing You hear the fears too deep for words.

You promise perfect peace, and I so desperately need it. But I know that to grasp it I have to let go of my own fears. I have to turn her well-being over to You. Truthfully that's where it should be. I can't help her from here. But You, God, You are everywhere and see everything. Who better to watch out for her welfare and keep her safe?

I'm choosing to trust You, no matter how hard it gets. When I weaken and begin to doubt again, remind me that You'll never abandon either of us. Amen

★ ★ ★

*When anxiety was great within me, Your consolation brought me joy.*

*Psalm 94:19 NIV*

# HELP ME BE JOYFUL

★　★　★

"Joy is the infallible sign of the presence of God."
*Pierre Teilhard de Chardin*

*Dear Lord,* help me be joyful while I wait for my loved one to return home from war. I feel badly when I'm happy or when I experience something he can't. I know that's not reasonable, but I don't know how to stop feeling this way. Show me that I'm not taking something away from him by feeling happy.

I want him to know life isn't the same without him here. But I also know he doesn't want me to be miserable and sad the entire time he's gone. Help me find a balance between missing him and carrying on in his absence.

Show me it's not disloyal to enjoy the people around me while he's gone. Help me keep the hearts and minds of our friends and family focused on my loved one and what he needs, never about what I need.

Give me the tools I need and the assurance I need to be strong. Don't add to his burden by allowing him to worry about me and how I'm coping while he's gone. Keep us both strong, and help the time pass quickly until we can be together again. Amen

★　★　★

*For You have been my help, and in the shadow of Your wings I sing for joy.*

*Psalm 63:7 NASB*

# HELP ME TO CONTINUE
# TO MOVE FORWARD

★ ★ ★

"If we only have the will to walk,
then God is pleased with our stumbles."

*C. S. Lewis*

*Dear Lord,* while I'm waiting for my loved one to return, don't let me waste time. Show me how I can continue to move forward with the things You want me to do with my life. It's so hard. All I want to do is put everything and everyone on hold until she gets home. But I know this isn't what she would want.

Be specific about the things You want me to accomplish during this time. Help me to focus on You. I feel like, compared to her sacrifice, my life is shallow, almost without meaning. Help me overcome those feelings.

I know there are things I need to do, important things that You have planned specifically for me. Give me the eyes to see the path You want me to take. Help me look beyond my circumstances and see others who need my help. Don't let me spend this time wishing for something else, but to value each day as a gift from You. I know there is a purpose for me right now; please make it clear to me. Then give me what I need to accomplish Your will. Amen

★ ★ ★

*People may make plans in their minds, but the Lord decides what they will do.*

*Proverbs 16:9 NCV*

# RESTORE MY SENSE OF FUN

★ ★ ★

"A little faith will bring your soul to heaven,
but a lot of faith will bring heaven to your soul."
*Dwight L. Moody*

*Dear Lord,* I used to be such a fun and outgoing person. Now I hardly ever smile. I feel guilty about enjoying life when he's so far from home and in harm's way.

I know he wouldn't want me to feel this way, but I don't know how to move past this. It just feels so wrong to have fun when he might be in danger. I feel like I'm stuck, unable to enjoy the things I used to, especially if they were things that we did together.

Help me understand how to recapture that sense of fun I used to have, even when someone I love is far away. I know I need to let go of the worry that I'm somehow taking something away from him when I have fun.

Don't let my loved one be afraid to share the times of joy he's experiencing while he's away. I think that's my biggest fear, that he's always unhappy where he is. Give us both the courage to share our loneliness but also moments of laughter that happen when we're apart. Amen

★ ★ ★

*You will go out in joy and be led forth in peace; the mountains and hills will burst into song before you, and all the trees of the field will clap their hands.*

*Isaiah 55:12 NIV*

# YOU PROVIDE HOPE
# TO THE HOPELESS

★ ★ ★

"The stars may fall, but God's promises will stand and be fulfilled."

*J. I. Packer*

*Dear Lord,* thank You for providing the hope I need to get through this difficult time. It's so hard to be parted from the one I love. It's even harder knowing the difficulties she's facing while she's so far away. But before I can drown in discouragement, You provide the hope I so desperately need to stay strong.

At times like this I feel like such a weakling, giving into fear and depression. But the Bible promises that when I'm weak, You are strong. I also know that You are providing the same hope to my soldier. When she is beat down by the circumstances around her, You are there, lending her Your strength. You lift her up with Your presence and instill hope where there should be no hope.

I refuse to give in to depression and fear; instead I'm planting both feet and choosing to believe Your promises. You are restoring my hope, reminding me that You are always with me, no matter what. As encouraging as that promise is, it means even more to me that You haven't abandoned my loved one.

Thank You for the hope You provide, and the love You show to each of us. Amen

★ ★ ★

*Then you will call on me and come and pray to me, and I will listen to you.*

*Jeremiah 29:12 NIV*

# OVERWHELMING LONELINESS

★　★　★

"Sometimes the sound of silence is
the most deafening sound of all."

*K. L. Toth*

*Dear Lord,* at times my loneliness overwhelms me. I miss my loved one so much. I want to feel his strong arms around me again. I want to know he's safe and that we're able to move forward again together.

Of course I miss him physically, but it's so much more than that. I miss the way we laugh about things that no one else understands. The way we can communicate with only a look. Most of all, I miss the way he can make me feel when he grins at me.

Please step in and help me cope with his absence. I don't want to be like this. I want to be strong. I want to be someone he can be proud of. Show me how to cope with the loneliness.

Give me things to keep my mind occupied. Most of all, make the days pass quickly. Fill my life with the things You want to accomplish through me and give me the strength to move forward, in spite of missing him. Amen

★　★　★

*Cast your cares on the Lord, and he will sustain you; he will never let the righteous be shaken.*

*Psalm 55:22 NIV*

# RELIEVE MY GUILT

★ ★ ★

"It is His joy that remains in us that makes our joy full."

*A. B. Simpson*

*Dear Lord,* it's such a beautiful day here today that I feel guilty. How can I enjoy anything when I know what my loved one is going through? When I say it out loud, it doesn't make sense. My suffering doesn't help her, I know, but it's what I feel. Help me get past this. Help me learn how to live with peace and even joy while the one I care about is at war.

I know You don't want me to stop living while she's away. And I also know that she doesn't want me to be miserable. But it feels so wrong when I'm happy and maybe she's not. I don't even really know how to ask You to fix this. I can't seem to sort it out in my own mind.

I know You're there with her, taking care of her and providing for her in ways I never could. I guess I'm asking for You to give me peace about her and about going on with life. I never want her to feel like we've moved beyond her. I want her to know she's constantly in our prayers, in our hearts, and in our thoughts. But I also don't want to be a burden or a drain on those around me. I want to be strong. Help me learn how to find a balance. Amen

★ ★ ★

*Call upon Me in the day of trouble; I shall rescue you, and you will honor Me.*

*Psalm 50:15 NASB*

# FILL ME UP WITH HOPE

★ ★ ★

"God is the only one who can make
the valley of trouble a door of hope."

*Catherine Marshall*

*Dear Lord,* fill me with hope during this time. I'm so scared while my loved one is away, and so worried about what might happen. As each day drags by, I'm more and more overwhelmed by the despair I feel.

At times I worry so much about the horrible possibilities I can't remember to hope for the good things to come. I'm afraid my loved one will discover what I'm feeling and I'll become just one more burden he has to bear. I don't want to be this way. I want to look forward with hope and joyful anticipation.

Give me the tools I need to change my attitude. Put other people around me who have been through this same thing and come out victorious. I need some concrete examples of hope, something to counteract what I'm feeling.

Use this time to teach me how to focus on You God, and on Your promises. I can't seem to focus on anything positive. Guard me from people who would add to my despair. Don't let me be overwhelmed with the news media, but instead keep my eyes firmly on You. I am choosing to put my hope in You. Amen

★ ★ ★

*Rejoice in hope; be patient in affliction; be persistent in prayer.*

*Romans 12:12 HCSB*

# PATIENCE

Waiting for someone we love to return home from war is difficult, but allowing God to gift us with patience can reveal more joy than we ever thought possible.

# THANK YOU FOR
# THE CHANGES I SEE IN ME

★  ★  ★

"Patience is bitter, but its fruit is sweet."

*Aristotle*

*Dear Lord,* truthfully the last thing I want to do is thank You for this time of waiting that I've had to endure. But as I look back on this time, I can see the changes that are taking place. I'm learning a lot about how to be content where I am, even if it's not a place I've chosen for myself.

As I've waited for my loved one to return, I've been forced to look beyond my circumstances and learn to recognize the blessings that happen every day.

Continue to open my eyes to blessings found as I continue to grow through this time of waiting. Show me the joy found in patience. When this is over, please don't let me go back to the way I was. I want to take what I've learned and continue to move forward, growing into a stronger person.

Don't let me waste this gift that You've given me by turning around and being impatient with others who are still learning this lesson. Most of all, make sure I continue to rely on You as heavily as I've had to during this time. Amen

★  ★  ★

*A patient person shows great understanding, but a quick-tempered one promotes foolishness.*

*Proverbs 14:29 HCSB*

# PATIENCE FOR
# MY LOVED ONE'S RETURN

★ ★ ★

"Patience is the ability to idle your motor
when you feel like stripping your gears."

*Barbara Johnson*

*Dear Lord,* I'm so tired of waiting for my loved one to come home. It seems like he's been in harm's way forever. I'm sick of worrying, of sleepless nights, and eternal days. I want him home safe, and I want it now!

Beyond that, the closer it gets for him to come home, the more fearful I get. All I can think of are those stories of soldiers who are just days away from coming home and then never make it. It seems crazy. After waiting for so long, the little time left should pass quickly, but I'm finding just the opposite is true.

Give me the ability to cope with the time that's left. Help me find ways to occupy my mind, and keep me focused on You. Don't let me give in to panic and defeat. Put people around me who understand, who have been through this before and who can help me understand why I feel this way.

Help me, Lord, to cope for these last few weeks. Renew my strength and my faith, and keep me from doubting. Amen

★ ★ ★

*Even before they call, I will answer; while they are still speaking, I will hear.*

*Isaiah 65:24 HCSB*

# MAKE ME WILLING TO WAIT

★   ★   ★

"Patience is the companion of wisdom."

*Augustine*

*Dear Lord,* the waiting is so hard for me. Ever since my loved one left, all I've done is wait. I've waited to receive word she arrived and waited to get her address so I could send her something. Now I'm always waiting to hear from her, and most of all I'm waiting for her to return home.

I don't know how to make the time pass in ways that seem normal. Some days leap from thing to thing, and others drag for an eternity. All the while I feel totally useless. It's like my world is reduced to the thoughts in my mind and my roller-coaster emotions.

Help me find balance. Give me the perspective I need to cope with these circumstances. It seems that my emotions are all centered on my loved one, how she's doing and whether or not she's safe.

I know You can provide me with the foundation and support I so desperately need. As soon as my feelings come into play, I'm once more overwhelmed. Show me how to center myself back on You, God. Guard my heart and direct my path in Your ways. Amen

★   ★   ★

*You enlarged my path under me; so my feet did not slip.*

*2 Samuel 22:37 NKJV*

# HELP ME BEAT BACK
# THE LONELINESS

★ ★ ★

"Silence, too, can be torture."

*Justina Chen*

*Dear Lord,* I try to stay busy, but at times the loneliness is just too much to bear. Help me get through these times. Help me understand why we have to endure things like this. I want my loved one home with me, safe and sound.

I want to beat this loneliness, but so often it just leads to despair. Please give me what I need to turn this despair into a stronger faith. Show me how to rely on You more.

Teach me how to let my attitude be dependent on You and not on my circumstances. Use this weakness to strengthen my relationship with You. Let me get to know You in a deeper and even more solid way. Allow me to experience how deep and how wide Your love truly is for me.

Make me an example of how You can work in the lives of those who stay focused on You. Give me the discipline I need to keep turning back to You, no matter how hard this time becomes. Amen

★ ★ ★

*When you pass through the waters, I will be with you. When you cross rivers, you will not drown. When you walk through fire, you will not be burned, nor will the flames hurt you.*

*Isaiah 43:2 NCV*

# LET ME CLING TO YOU

★ ★ ★

"Sorrow looks back. Worry looks around. Faith looks up."

*Ralph Waldo Emerson*

*Dear Lord,* I'm struggling right now. I want to pray for my loved one, but the words won't come. Even when I can get the words out, my prayers just seem to hit the ceiling and bounce back down. I want to feel like You're listening, but You seem so far away. Lord, come close. Show me You're here.

Give me something to hold that I can trust. Give me a tangible way to know You're listening. Please strengthen my faith. I'm so weak, and I'm afraid my prayers for my loved one are ineffective. I know the power to keep her safe doesn't come from me, but the words I pray seem so hopeless.

Show me how to pray when I have no words. Remind others to pray for my loved one. Bring her to the minds and thoughts of people who know her. And then, please give me the comfort of knowing others are praying for her. Most of all remind me of Your faithfulness, even when I'm weak. Amen

★ ★ ★

*In the same way, the Spirit helps us in our weakness. We do not know what we ought to pray for, but the Spirit himself intercedes for us through wordless groans.*

*Romans 8:26 NIV*

# TRUSTING GOD FOR EVERYTHING

★  ★  ★

"Quit questioning God and start trusting Him!"

*Joel Osteen*

*Dear Lord,* I'm scared. I want to know that my loved one is okay. I want to believe You'll keep him safe, but I don't know how to truly trust that idea. The fear I feel lodges in my heart, blocking out all hope. Give me a sign that I can trust You. Show me how to find the hope I once had.

Show me what trust looks like by giving me an example of someone who trusts You. Let me feel Your presence around me, so I know You'll be real to my soldier and be with him. Point out examples of how You've proved trustworthy in the past, so I can apply them to the future.

Give me friends who understand, and don't make me feel badly when I don't trust like I should. Let me get to know You on a deeper level through this so that You become my foundation and I trust You without doubting.

As I struggle to find the words to pray, send others to pray in my place. Show me how You've already provided what I need and especially what my loved one needs. Teach me how to trust You with his well-being. Show me that You are there when I need You. Amen

★  ★  ★

*Those who know your name trust in you, for you, Lord, have never forsaken those who seek you.*

*Psalm 9:10 NIV*

# HELP ME WITH THE SMALL STUFF

★ ★ ★

"By perseverance the snail reached the ark."

*Charles H Spurgeon*

*Dear Lord,* some days the small details of life overwhelm me. Truthfully, they are harder to bear than the big stuff. It seems like every appliance breaks while my loved one is gone. Please protect me from the myriad of small disasters that come thick and fast during a deployment.

All the decisions we made together now fall to me. I feel so inadequate. It often feels like I'm trying to operate with only half a brain. Be there for me, God. Give me the knowledge I need to handle all of this. Show me clearly when I can do something myself or when I need to ask someone else for help.

I hate to impose on others. Please give me the courage to ask for help when I need it. I know everyone has a full schedule, and they don't need to worry about me. I should be able to handle the day-to-day details of life. But there are times when I just can't.

Put people in my life who can anticipate those times. Make them bold to speak up and offer to help. Amen

★ ★ ★

*And let us not grow weary while doing good, for in due season we shall reap if we do not lose heart.*

*Galatians 6:9 NKJV*

# HELP, I'M TOTALLY OVERWHELMED

★ ★ ★

"Our greatest glory is not in never failing,
but in rising up every time we fail."

*Ralph Waldo Emerson*

*Dear Lord,* I'm overwhelmed right now with thoughts of my loved one. I miss him so much. All I want to do is hide somewhere safe and not show my face until he's back home.

I know I need to be strong. I'm stuck inside a storm of emotions. I just want to feel his arms around me and hear his voice whisper how much he loves me. The time until his return stretches out so long in front of me that I can't see the end.

At times, my life feels empty, and I struggle to reconnect with my purpose. I want to think being strong matters, but with him gone nothing seems to matter. Show me what does matter and then help me to focus. Don't let me become just one more burden for my loved one to bear.

Help me cope with the loneliness. Give me the tools, the people, the things I need to be able to go on. I didn't know it was possible to cry yourself out of tears, but that's just what I've done. Let me feel Your presence. Show me You're here with me. Give me the strength to hang on. Amen

★ ★ ★

*Lord, hear my prayer; listen to my cry for mercy. Answer me because you are loyal and good.*

*Psalm 143:1 NCV*

# FAITH

Trusting God to take care of people we love is hard enough when they're close by. Turning their well-being over to Him when they're at war takes strength beyond imagining. God is able to give us that strength and grow our faith—all while He's keeping those we love safe from harm.

# HELP ME HANG ON

★ ★ ★

"Fear is faithlessness."

*George MacDonald*

*Dear Lord,* I'm trying to stay positive for my loved one's sake, but inside I'm slipping. I can feel myself tumbling into a pit of depression.

Replace my negative thoughts with faith. Help me turn off the litany of what can go wrong and replace those images with Your promises. Lord, I know You can bring her home safely, and I know that when I rely on You, I'm strong. But at times I don't want to be strong. I just want to bury my head and cry.

I want to lash out at a world filled with other loved ones who aren't in harm's way. I want to scream that it's not fair. It's not that I want other young men and women in danger; I just want my loved one to be safe at home.

Show me how to guard my thoughts and to process all the things I'm feeling. Let me accept help from my friends instead of hiding away and feeling sorry for myself. Most of all, wrap my loved one and me in Your loving arms and carry us safely through this difficult time. Amen

★ ★ ★

*The Lord is close to the brokenhearted and saves those who are crushed in spirit.*

*Psalm 34:18 NIV*

# STRENGTHEN MY FAITH

★　★　★

"Faith gives you an inner strength and
a sense of balance and perspective in life."

*Gregory Peck*

*Dear Lord,* I'm so afraid for my loved one during this time of deployment. It seems the harder I try not to think about all the bad things that could happen, the more they fill my mind. I dread time spent by myself and especially times when I try to sleep. The images that fill my mind won't leave me alone.

You are my source of comfort, and I need Your strength to get through this. I want to be strong, but I'm not. I don't have anywhere to turn for help, except You. But I know You are my help and are faithful to answer when I call.

I always thought I had all the faith I needed, but I don't. Having a loved one deployed has shown me otherwise. I realize my faith is weak, and now, when I desperately need it, it won't support me. Help me strengthen it into something that will carry me through these circumstances.

Be my provider, and the one who protects me from myself. Amen

★　★　★

*He heals the brokenhearted and binds up their wounds.*

*Psalm 147:3 HCSB*

# GROW MY FAITH

★ ★ ★

"Faith is like an empty, open hand stretched out towards God,
with nothing to offer and everything to receive."

*John Calvin*

*Dear Lord,* I want to be strong for my family and especially for
my soldier, but I know I can't until I learn to lean on You. Teach me
what I need to know.

Use this situation to grow my faith. Show me in Your Word the
passages I need to hold on to when I am afraid. Surround me with
Your children who will pray for me when I can't pray for myself.
Help me learn to lean on You when things get difficult and not try
to do everything by myself. You promise to be with me, no matter
what. Give me that opportunity.

Teach me to turn to You in all my situations, no matter how
easy and especially no matter how hard. I know You love me with
a feeling so deep it can't be contained. I want to experience that
abundant love for myself.

Turn my thoughts to You when I'm weak. Don't let my despair
keep me from experiencing You to the fullest. I'm lonely and I'm
worried about my loved one. Show me how You can bring triumph
out of tragedy when I rely You. Amen

★ ★ ★

*Therefore, do not throw away your confidence, which has a great
reward.*

*Hebrews 10:35 NASB*

# GIVE ME THE FAITH
# TO PRAY AND BELIEVE

★ ★ ★

"A perfect faith would lift us absolutely above fear."

*George MacDonald*

*Dear Lord,* I worry so much about my loved one's safety. Everyday, the thoughts of him lying injured or worse crowd out my ability to pray. Please, please keep him safe. Guard him with everything You have.

I worry that my prayers aren't passionate enough, or that I'm not good enough for You to hear. I want to bargain, to beg, to plead, but I have such little faith at times that all I can do is cry. I know the Bible says You love him more than I do, but how can that be? I've spent so much of my life protecting him, and now I'm powerless.

Give me Your peace. Let me see evidence of Your love for him. I know it in my mind, but my heart is broken, and I can't find that evidence in the pieces. Help me remember those times when You intervened and kept us from tragedy. Bring back the memories that prove Your love over and over.

Put people in our lives who will pray for my loved one when I can't. Reassure me, through them, that You haven't forgotten us and that we matter to You. Remind me of the price You paid to keep us safe, to give us a future and a hope. Calm my fears and take the burden off my shoulders and replace it with Your perfect peace. Amen

★ ★ ★

*Relieve the troubles of my heart and free me from my anguish.*

*Psalm 25:17 NIV*

# THANK YOU THAT YOU HEAR AND ANSWER OUR PRAYERS

★ ★ ★

"We serve a God who is waiting to hear from you,
and He can't wait to respond."

*Priscilla Shirer*

*Dear Lord,* I don't know how I'd make it through this time if I didn't have You. But I do have You, and You are a God of answered prayers. No matter how big or how small, my concerns become Yours.

You are faithful to care about the people and things that I care about. I can bring You my burdens and lay them at Your feet. I can leave them there, knowing that You will take care of each one. This is such a comfort, especially now, as I face the situation of having someone I care about serving in a war zone.

So often, the things I worry about seem to have no good answer. But I've learned that I don't have to have an answer for You to provide what's needed. In every situation You already know what is best for each of us. I know this is true because I've watched so many impossible situations turn out in a way that none could have imagined.

Thank You for hearing and answering my prayers. Amen

★ ★ ★

*Therefore I say to you, whatever things you ask when you pray, believe that you receive them, and you will have them.*

*Mark 11:24 NKJV*

# RUNNING LOW ON FAITH

★　★　★

"Where reason cannot wade, there faith may swim."

*Thomas Watson*

*Dear Lord,* You are so faithful to me, even when I'm weak. You promise to be strong when I'm not. I need Your strength right now. I'm running low on faith, and I need You to step in and help me.

I lie in bed at night, missing my loved one and wondering what dangers he's facing now. I can't sleep because of the worry and fear I feel for him. I know You love him even more than I do, but sometimes that doesn't even seem possible. Help me to remember that he was Yours before he was mine and will be Yours long after I am gone. Help me learn to trust You more. Grow my faith so it will sustain me when the fear and doubts creep in.

He's facing things I don't even want to imagine, much less give voice to, but the images just won't go away. In my nightmares, I see him in trouble, calling out to me, and I can't get to him. Protect me from these thoughts. Take control of my mind, and show me how to control my thoughts.

Give me the courage to let go of my worry and instead rely on You to protect him, no matter what happens. Use this time to make me stronger and to grow my faith until I can confidently tell the world You are the One in whom I place my trust. Amen

★　★　★

*"But blessed is the one who trusts in the Lord, whose confidence is in him."*

*Jeremiah 17:7 NIV*

# GIVE ME THE FAITH I NEED TO STAND FIRM

★ ★ ★

"Faith is not belief without proof, but trust without reservation."

*Elton Trueblood*

*Dear Lord,* I want to believe You're there with my loved one, but it's so hard to let go of the fear. I love her so much and want her to be safe. I need to learn how to have faith. Help me release her protection into Your loving hands.

I really do know You love her, even more than I do. It's irrational, but I feel like she'll be in more danger if I stop worrying about her. Give me the courage to have faith in You. Show me how to learn to trust You.

I measure the passage of time by the contact I have with her. I live for the moments when I know for sure she's safe. This isn't what she'd want for me, and I know it's not Your plan for me, God. Help me turn her well-being over to You.

You know everything. The Bible says You know the beginning from the end. That means You know what dangers lie in her path. Give her what she needs to know what's ahead. Guard her in all ways and at all times. Then give me a glimpse of how You're working to keep her safe. Forgive my lack of faith, but help me see the proof of how strong You are. I'm choosing now to believe You are there with her. Give me the faith to stand firm. Amen

★ ★ ★

*You, therefore, my son, be strong in the grace that is in Christ Jesus.*

*2 Timothy 2:1 HCSB*

# LEAD ME INTO HOPE

★  ★  ★

"Hope is faith in seed form—faith is hope in final form."

*Rex Rouis*

*Dear Lord,* I'm so tired of living with the fear of what might happen while my loved one is on deployment. I need You to replace it with hope. It seems that the closer I get to her homecoming, the more hopeless and fearful I become. I can't continue to live like this. It isn't good for me or for anyone around me.

You promise us that hope is found in You. I'm turning to You right now. I need to learn what being hopeful looks like in this situation. It's so hard to let go and put my hope in anything at this moment, even You. I'm ashamed to admit that, but it's true. I need Your help.

Give me something tangible to hold on to. Remind me of a time when You've protected the one I love and kept her safe. Put someone in my life who has faced this kind of struggle and found a way to let go. Give me a companion who understands and will help me move forward. Strengthen my faith so I can let go of the fear.

I want to trust You, to put my faith in You, but it's so hard. Hold me close, give me Your peace, and lead me to Your hope. Amen

★  ★  ★

*Trust in the Lord with all your heart, and lean not on your own understanding; in all your ways acknowledge Him, and He shall direct your paths.*

*Proverbs 3:5-6 NKJV*

# STRENGTH

In the same way we worry about those at war, they worry about those left at home. Asking God to strengthen us can relieve that burden and help them focus on the job they've been given.

# SHOW ME HOW TO BE STRONG

★ ★ ★

"Real true faith is man's weakness leaning on God's strength."
*Dwight L. Moody*

*Dear Lord,* I'm running low on strength, and I can't afford that. I need to be strong for those around me and especially for my soldier. The last thing he needs is for me to be weak and add to his worries. But I want him back home, and I want it now.

I'm tired of pretending to be strong when all I want to do is crawl in a corner and not come out until he's back home safely. I want to be strong—to have a strong faith. But I need help. I know I'm not even close to being that person.

Give me an example of what it means to be strong and full of faith. Does everyone in this situation just fake it, or is there really a way to do more than just hang on? At this point I don't see how it can be done.

I can feel myself pulling away from those who want to help me, but I'm afraid if they get too close, they'll see what a mess I am. Help me find a way out of this. I desperately need Your perspective and Your truth in this.

In the Bible I've read that You give strength to the weak and hope to the hopeless. Well, that describes me perfectly. Give me what I need so I can do more than just cope but can be someone my loved one can be proud of. Amen

★ ★ ★

*I can do all things through Christ, because he gives me strength.*
*Philippians 4:13 NCV*

# THANK YOU FOR SHARING YOUR STRENGTH WITH ME

★ ★ ★

"I wouldn't choose it, but I wouldn't change it."

*Edie Melson*

*Dear Lord,* I know that there's no way I'd be able to get through these times of deployment without Your strength to sustain me. Having someone I love so far away, in harm's way, has taught me what true strength really is.

It's like I had been going through life with my right arm tied behind my back. I was weak, and I didn't even realize it. As hard as this has been, and continues to be, I wouldn't trade what I've learned for anything.

I pray it's a lesson that I'll never forget and one that I'll share with others who are also struggling. This time has grown me in ways I never could have imagined. I've experienced the height and depth of Your love for me and for my soldier, as You've surrounded us with Your love and carried us with Your strength.

★ ★ ★

*But He said to me, "My grace is sufficient for you, for power is perfected in weakness." Therefore, I will most gladly boast all the more about my weaknesses, so that Christ's power may reside in me.*

*2 Corinthians 12:9 HCSB*

# CARRY ME WHEN I'M WEAK

★ ★ ★

"I am mended by my sickness, enriched by my poverty,
and strengthened by my weakness."

*Abraham Wright*

*Dear Lord,* I just feel empty. I don't have any emotions, or prayers, or even any hope. I'm tired of waiting, tired of asking, tired of trying to stay strong. All I want to do is curl up in a corner and hide until my loved one comes home.

I don't want to go through the motions of pretending to be something I'm not. Lord, I need You to carry me. At times, even drawing a breath seems like too much work. Can You fill me up? Can You give me the will to carry on and to be brave for my family?

The Bible promises when we cry out, You are faithful to answer us. What if we haven't been faithful to You for a long time? Will You still come? I'm choosing to believe You will. In spite of the emptiness, I do feel Your love. I can sense that You want me to have peace, want me to not give up. Show me I'm not imagining this.

Until I can get back up, lend me Your strength. Show me the way back to hope. Hold me close until I can stand on my own. Don't abandon me to the depths of my despair. And when I come out of this victorious, give me the words to tell others about how You helped me in my darkest hours. Amen

★ ★ ★

*In their misery they cried out to the Lord, and he saved them from their troubles.*

*Psalm 107:28 NCV*

# THE POWER OF PRAYER

★ ★ ★

"You are no stronger than your belief system."

*T. D. Jakes*

*Dear Lord,* I need Your help too. I want to be strong for my loved one as he serves and for my family. But once again, I'm just a mess. All I can think about are his miserable conditions and my inability to help him. I've read that the most powerful thing I can do is pray. But prayer doesn't feel powerful. It feels like the least I can do.

Show me the power of prayer. Teach me to trust You to take care of my loved one and keep him safe. Provide for his every need in ways that exceed anything I would have ever considered.

More than anything, I want to help him. But I feel so powerless, and life is so out of control. So often I wonder if I'm even praying the right way.

Give me the strength to believe You will hear and answer my prayers. Give me the faith to keep on praying even when it feels like it isn't doing any good at all. Teach me to trust You and rely on You completely when it comes to keeping my loved one safe.

I really do know it's never been about what I can do but only what You can do. Keep reminding me of that until I never forget. Please remind him that You really are all he needs. Amen

★ ★ ★

*Pray without ceasing.*

*1 Thessalonians 5:17 NASB*

# HELP ME TAKE CARE OF MY HEALTH

★ ★ ★

"It is important to get out of your own way."
*Ray Bradbury*

*Dear Lord,* I'm praying for my own strength as I wait for my loved one to come home from war. She's fighting battles where she is, and I'm fighting them here. I struggle with maintaining healthy eating habits. Nothing feels right while my loved one is in danger.

Help me stay focused on keeping myself healthy. Give me the strength to make wise choices for what I eat and drink. Bring others around to encourage me to stay on a regular exercise routine. I don't want to add to my soldier's burden by getting sick while she's gone.

As much as I struggle with getting enough exercise, I'm also having trouble with getting enough sleep every night. This makes me tired during the day, which affects my motivation to exercise and that affects my appetite. I seem to be on a downward spiral.

Please break in and help me focus and be strong. I don't want to give my loved one more thing to worry about. I know if she saw me like this she would be concerned. Give me the strength I need to pull myself together. Help me have the courage to reach out to friends and family who can help me fight this battle. Amen

★ ★ ★

*He sent His word and healed them, and delivered them from their destructions.*

*Psalm 107:20 NASB*

# LEND ME YOUR STRENGTH

★ ★ ★

"Courage is resistance to fear, mastery of fear—
not absence of fear."

*Mark Twain*

*Dear Lord,* I'm worn out. I'm exhausted by the worry and fear that I've let dominate my life since my loved one's been at war on top of all my normal responsibilities. Those emotions are influencing almost everything in my life. I don't want to get out or participate in anything enjoyable, and I don't want anyone around me.

I know I can't go on like this. I'm making myself sick and depressed by allowing my focus to turn to all the negatives in my life. At this point, even though I desperately need to change, I don't know if I can. I truly don't have the energy, and I don't know where to start.

My family is worried about me, and I know that if my loved one discovers what a wreck I am, he'll be worried as well. The last thing he needs right now is to worry about his family.

Help me turn my focus back to You. Help me once again find joy in day-to-day life. Replace my fear with peace, and keep me from worry. Don't leave me in this condition, but take my hand and lead me back into the light. Amen

★ ★ ★

*"The Lord is my strength and song, and He has become my salvation; This is my God, and I will praise Him; my father's God, and I will extol Him."*

*Exodus 15:2 NASB*

# I DON'T KNOW HOW TO BE STRONG

★ ★ ★

"Deny your weakness, and you will
never realize God's strength in you."

*Joni Eareckson Tada*

*Dear Lord,* help me take an interest in the things around me again. I'm torn with wanting to not disappoint my family and just wanting to put life on hold until my loved one comes back home from war.

I don't want to do anything without her here. I hate holidays, birthdays, and any special occasion because it just points to the fact that my loved one isn't here to celebrate with us. But it's not fair to everyone else. They shouldn't have to put their lives on hold.

Beyond that, I know my soldier would want us to continue on with normal life. She knows we'll have lots of celebrations when she comes back home. But when I go on with my life, it feels like I'm neglecting her or taking something away from her by feeling happy. Just saying it out loud makes me shake my head at how ridiculous that notion is. Yet I still can't shake the feeling.

Help me. Show me how to continue on with life and still honor my loved one's service and sacrifice. I feel like I'm caught between two polar opposites. Give me Your perspective and Your wisdom on how to be strong while she's away. Amen

★ ★ ★

*Splendor and majesty are before Him; strength and joy are in His place.*

*1 Chronicles 16:27 NASB*

# HELP ME FINANCIALLY

★ ★ ★

"God never gives us anything to do that he
does not give us the strength to do."

*Jack Hyles*

*Dear Lord,* some days the burden of being in charge of this family without my loved one is more than I can stand. I just don't see how we can make it financially until he returns. Everywhere I turn the expenses grow. The car breaks down, the appliances quit, and the money just isn't enough.

Is this what You had in mind when You let him leave for war? We're already sacrificing so much, why can't things work out financially? The Bible says that You're all we need. I've always thought I believed that, but now I see how shallow my understanding has been.

Lord I need You to show up in a big way, and soon. I'm out of resources, and my faith is almost gone. Send someone to help us. Give me the tools I need to keep things afloat here at home. Use this time to show me what it means to rely on You no matter what. Help me so I don't add to my loved one's burden. I know he's worried about us, and that's the last thing he needs. Provide for this family in our time of need. Amen

★ ★ ★

*It is the blessing of the Lord that makes rich, And He adds no sorrow to it.*

*Proverbs 10:22 NASB*

# ANGER

Anger can be a natural result of living with a loved one in danger. When we turn our fears over to God, He will step in and help us cope with the emotional reactions that can overwhelm us.

# DON'T LET ME RESENT
# MY LOVED ONE'S SERVICE

★ ★ ★

"Hot heads and cold hearts never solved anything."
*Billy Graham*

*Dear Lord,* while my loved one serves, protect our marriage. I know it would be so easy for both of us to misunderstand words and intentions. Keep us focused on making our marriage even stronger because of going through these difficult times.

It's so hard being apart. The times when I get to hear his voice are few. While I long for them, those times can be so bittersweet. Hearing him just makes me want him beside me even more.

Help me remember why he's chosen to serve. Remind me that these times are just as hard on him and that he hates being apart as much as me. I know this willingness to sacrifice is a big part of who You made him to be. And it's a huge part of why I love him so much.

Make sure that the times we do get to talk aren't filled with awkward silences but instead fly by because we have so much to share and say. Don't let others tear down our relationship while we're apart. Surround us both with people who will encourage us to stay strong and focused on our commitment. Most of all, help us both grow closer together as we grow closer to You. Amen

★ ★ ★

*Forget about the wrong things people do to you, and do not try to get even. Love your neighbor as you love yourself. I am the Lord.*

*Leviticus 19:18 NCV*

# GIVE ME ASSURANCE ABOUT
# MY LOVED ONE'S SAFETY

★ ★ ★

"Do not build up obstacles in your imagination.
Difficulties must be studied and dealt with,
but they must not be magnified by fear."

*Norman Vincent Peale*

*Dear Lord,* give me the assurance I need about how well my loved one is doing while she's away. I worry about her so much. The long nights are the worst. When I close my eyes, I can still feel how empty the other side of the bed is. Then, my mind fills with images of her lying somewhere alone injured or worse. When sleep does finally come, it's littered with my voiceless fears about the one I love.

I know the Bible says You love her even more than I do, but I can't seem to translate that knowledge into a sense of peace. Show me how to trust You and let go of my fears.

Let me hear from her regularly, through letters, phone calls, and the Internet. I need to see for myself that she's whole and well. As much as I fear for her physical safety, I worry about her stress level. I need You to show me she's coping with what she's going through during this deployment. I worry about her coming back to us filled with anger and bitterness about what she's experienced. Give me what I need to make it through as well. Amen

★ ★ ★

*I have set the Lord continually before me; because He is at my right hand, I will not be shaken.*

*Psalm 16:8 NASB*

# YOU WILL BE FOUND
# BY THOSE WHO SEEK YOU

★ ★ ★

"God is in the darkness and God is in the wilderness.
I now know that by personal experience."

*Anne Graham Lotz*

*Dear Lord,* I am so thankful that You are not limited by time and space. You are faithful and make Yourself available to all who call upon Your great and mighty name. I don't have to worry that the soldier I love is too far for You to reach, even if he is far from me.

I know You will provide him what he needs the very moment he needs it. Your faithfulness to walk with him isn't dependent on anything he does or anything I do.

There have been times while we've been apart that I didn't think I could go on. Whenever those feelings of hopelessness have hit, I've been aware of Your presence, supporting and comforting me. You reassure me when I doubt and lose heart. I know You are doing the exact same thing for my soldier. Thank You for Your presence, no matter what comes our way. Amen

★ ★ ★

*And without faith it is impossible to please Him, for he who comes to God must believe that He is and that He is a rewarder of those who seek Him.*

*Hebrews 11:6 NASB*

# TAKE AWAY MY ANGER
# AT THE ENEMY

★  ★  ★

"Snuggle in God's arms. When you are hurting,
when you feel lonely, left out. Let him cradle you, comfort you,
reassure you of his all-sufficient power and love."

*Kay Arthur*

*Dear Lord,* don't let my anger get the better of me. At times, this situation makes me so mad that I don't know how to cope. It's not fair that this enemy is causing my loved one to put her life on the line. Their ignorance, their hatred isn't something I know how to deal with.

How can I not be angry at them? How do I not return their hatred with my own? I know, in my head, that this is where You come in. You've promised to teach me to love the unlovable. I need to learn that lesson fast.

When I see someone who reminds me of the enemy my soldier is fighting, I want to lash out and cause them the hurt I feel. I desperately need Your help. I'm to the point where I want You to take this anger away. I'm tired of carrying the weight of resentment.

Teach me how to return their hatred with love. I know I don't have the capacity to love them. Will You love them through me? Let me see these people as You do. Amen

★  ★  ★

*A hot-tempered man stirs up strife, but the slow to anger calms a dispute.*

*Proverbs 15:18 NASB*

189

# HELP ME NOT MEET
# IGNORANCE WITH ANGER

★ ★ ★

"Angry people are not always wise."

*Jane Austen*

*Dear Lord,* I'm so tired of dealing with people who say hurtful things when they think they're being kind or who just say things without thinking at all. I'm sick of people who think I may be disappointed in the life choices my loved one has made. I'm worried about him, and I wish he wasn't fighting in a war. But I'm proud that he's chosen to sacrifice and serve as a soldier.

I think what frustrates me most is what I see and hear in the media. I'm especially angered by those who think protesting at a military base or even worse, a military funeral, can effect a positive change. The people affected by those protests have no power to make the changes needed.

Help me channel my anger into constructive ways. Make me an instrument of change and an ambassador of peace to those who express themselves in hurtful ways. Most of all, don't let me become like them and react in anger. Amen

★ ★ ★

*"In your anger do not sin." Do not let the sun go down while you are still angry.*

*Ephesians 4:26 NIV*

# TAKE AWAY MY ANGER AT YOU

★ ★ ★

"Past tears are present strength."
*George MacDonald*

*Dear Lord,* as I tried to pray today, I realized where the majority of my anger is coming from. I'm mad at You, even as I admit this I'm filled with fear. I'm so ashamed that I feel this way, but I can't ignore what I'm feeling any longer.

Everything is so mixed up in my mind and my emotions. You are God, Creator of the universe. Because You are all-powerful, I know You could put an end to this. I also know that You love each of us with a depth that we truly cannot wrap our minds around. I just cannot reconcile these two things in my mind.

I'm turning to You for help. I know my feelings come from the fact that I like to be in control. What I'm really finding out during this time is that I never was in control. It's so hard to turn my loved one's well-being over to anyone else, even You, God! Admitting that scares me. I want You to help my soldier, and I don't want You to be angry with me.

I've read the Bible. I know You're not petty and vengeful. Instead, You are a God who blesses and who spreads out His arms to protect. Forgive me for my feelings, and help me move past them. Amen

★ ★ ★

*God, create a clean heart for me and renew a steadfast spirit within me.*
*Psalm 51:10 HCSB*

# HELP ME CHANNEL MY ANGER INTO SOMETHING GOOD

★ ★ ★

"For every minute you remain angry,
you give up sixty seconds of peace of mind."

*Ralph Waldo Emerson*

*Dear Lord,* at times I'm so angry about the situation we're in. It's not fair that my loved one is serving when so many others aren't. I know it was his choice, but at times I don't understand why more aren't willing to make that sacrifice. Can't they see the need we have?

Then, when I hear derogatory remarks about our military, I get so mad. I don't know how to answer or even whether I should answer. I really just want this world to be different, and I want to be an instrument of change.

How do I work to make the world better when all I want to do is lash out to those around me? I desperately need Your perspective on this. I know there's nothing that promises life will be fair, but it's still what I want.

Give me the tools I need to let go of these destructive emotions. Replace them with some real, constructive things I can do to make a difference. Show me how to return love when I'm faced with hate. Help me make the same kind of sacrifices here at home that my loved one is making while he's at war. Amen

★ ★ ★

*Refrain from anger and turn from wrath; do not fret—it leads only to evil.*

*Psalm 37:8 NIV*

# HELP ME OVERCOME ANGER

★  ★  ★

"God is more interested in your future and
your relationships than you are."
*Billy Graham*

*Dear Lord,* help me not be overcome by the anger I feel. The last thing I ever wanted was for my loved one to have to fight in a war. Yet that's exactly where she is. I'm so frustrated and find myself wanting to lash out at everyone because of where she is and what she's doing. Can't they see her sacrifice and that it's for them?

I'm mad at our government for getting us in this situation. I'm mad at others who didn't volunteer to serve in the military. Even though I'm ashamed to admit it, I'm also mad at my loved one. I am proud of what she's doing, but I don't understand why she felt she needed to be the one who sacrificed. My emotions are so mixed up.

I know I'm not supposed to be, but I'm also angry with You, God. There's no point in hiding it, You already know how I'm feeling. I just don't know what to do with all this rage. It's poisoning my relationships with friends and family. I desperately need Your perspective. I need a way to process what I'm feeling. I want to go back to trusting You like a little child, instead of doubting that You have everything well in hand. Did You feel this way when Jesus sacrificed everything? Help me understand this from Your perspective. Amen

★  ★  ★

*"For My thoughts are not your thoughts, nor are your ways My ways."*
*declares the Lord.*

*Isaiah 55:8 NASB*

# REACHING OUT
# TO OTHERS

Sometimes the only way to get some needed perspective on our situation is to reach out to others. Often the added benefit is the comfort and wisdom they bring to us.

# LEAD ME TO HELP OTHERS

★  ★  ★

"Alone we can do so little; together we can do so much."

*Helen Keller*

*Dear Lord,* while my loved one is deployed, I'm asking You to direct my steps here at home. I want to help him in any way possible, but there are very limited things I can do. I know I can pray. I've read that prayer is the most powerful thing I can do, but I still long to take action even beyond that.

I'm asking that You would direct me to other people who are struggling with loved ones deployed, and give me the opportunity to reach out to them. Use me as a way to keep the sacrifices of the men and women in the military at the forefront of people's thoughts and prayers.

Lead others to me so we can come together to support each other and pray for our family members who are fighting in a war so far away. Give me eyes to recognize others in this situation as I go about my daily life. Put people in my path, and help them have the courage to reach out. Always remind me that You are present and watching out for us all. Amen

★  ★  ★

*Your word is a lamp for my feet, a light on my path.*

*Psalm 119:105 NIV*

# USE ME TO HELP OTHERS WHO ARE HURTING

★ ★ ★

"Focus on giving smiles away, and you will always discover
that your own smiles will always be in great supply!"

*Joyce Meyer*

*Dear Lord,* I'm amazed at how much You love me. I've needed You so much while my loved one's been gone, and You've been here. It's been a struggle, but I've been able to watch You at work. I've seen and experienced the concrete proof of how much You love each of us.

Now I'm asking You to give me the opportunity to use the lessons I've learned to help someone else who's hurting. I know what it's like to lie awake at night, so worried about my loved one that I'm afraid to close my eyes. More than that, I know what it's like to turn that worry and fear over to You and feel Your peace wash away the terror.

Give me the eyes I need to spot others who are in pain and facing separation. Help me have the courage to reach out. Don't let me turn back when life gets hard, but keep me focused on You in all things. Amen

★ ★ ★

*The righteous person may have many troubles, but the Lord delivers him from them all.*

*Psalm 34:19 NIV*

# HELP ME ENCOURAGE OTHERS

★ ★ ★

"The language of friendship is not words but meanings."
*Henry David Thoreau*

*Dear Lord,* You have given me so many reasons to be thankful. I want to be a source of strength and encouragement to others. You've put people in my life to pray for my loved one while he's at war, as well as people to lift me up when I'm down. Now I want to do that for others.

Give me the opportunity to reach out to others who are in similar circumstances. Let me share with them the hope You've given me. I know I haven't arrived. There are times when I still despair. But it's always easier to cope if I'm not focusing on myself.

Help me to see others who need a friend. Let me spot them as I go about my daily life. Beyond that, let them come to me and ask for help, and don't ever let me turn someone down who needs help.

No matter what happens, use me as a source of joy for others who are struggling. Make me more faithful to pray for those in need and a better friend to any who are hurting.

Let me be an example of how You can work through our difficult circumstances. Let me be Your victory over doubt for someone else. Amen

★ ★ ★

*Restore the joy of Your salvation to me, and give me a willing spirit. Then I will teach the rebellious Your ways, and sinners will return to You.*

*Psalm 51:12-13 HCSB*

# HELP ME DEVELOP JOYFUL ANTICIPATION

★ ★ ★

"We could never learn to be brave and patient,
if there were only joy in the world."

*Helen Keller*

*Dear Lord,* give me the patience and strength to see this deployment through. The days apart stretch so far that it seems like my loved one will never get to come back home. The more I want time to pass quickly, the slower it seems to go. Help me learn to have patience and develop joyful anticipation.

Patience is so hard for me. Please change my attitude. Show me the joy that can be found in living each day to the fullest, instead of wishing them away weeks at a time.

I hate being apart from my loved one. But I know You have promised to bring good out of even the worst situations. Help me see the good that's happening right now.

Don't let me miss what You have for me today in the rush to get to tomorrow. Surround me with others who have mastered this valuable lesson, and give them what they need to show me what they've learned. Give me the tools to do more than just cope. Guide me into the victory You have for me over impatience. Amen

★ ★ ★

*If you remain in me and my words remain in you, ask whatever you wish, and it will be done for you.*

*John 15:7 NIV*

# THANK YOU THAT YOU ARE
# A GOD OF JOY AND BLESSINGS

★　★　★

*"Good humor and laughter are far too wonderful*
*not to come straight from the heart of God."*

*Beth Moore*

*Dear Lord,* today I want to take time to thank You. No matter what we're going through, it's abundantly clear that You truly are a God of joy and blessings. I know my soldier has a difficult job to do, but I also know You are there with him.

You give him the joy he needs to be able to carry on. Your blessings come to each of us with the unexpectedness of a parent surprising a child. Even if I can't be there to help shoulder the burden of my loved one, I can be confident that You are.

I know that the joy You provide goes deeper than just momentary happiness. It begins as an inward warmth of the heart, working its way outward until it covers everything with the perspective of a God who cares for us with an infinite love.

Even though my soldier is in the midst of great stress and even danger, I know You are giving him moments of joy to sustain him.

Thank You for giving him what he needs, even before I can ask. Amen

★　★　★

*The Lord is my shepherd, I shall not want.*

*Psalm 23:1 NASB*

# GIVE US UNITY ACROSS THE MILES

★ ★ ★

"A marriage is the union of two good forgivers."
*Ruth Bell Graham*

*Dear Lord,* I feel the miles between me and my loved one in so many ways. It's more than just the physical separation that's weighing on me; it's the gulf between us emotionally. We seem to be going in different directions. We've lost our unity, and I'm begging You to restore it.

In the past, we've always known how the other was feeling, and almost what we were each thinking. Now I'm blind to what's happening with my loved one. Trying to talk over the Internet and on an international phone line doesn't help. The time delays seem to lead to nothing but awkward pauses and misunderstandings.

Help us to return to the way we were. I can't stand this disconnect between us. Show what I need to understand a little of what she's going through.

Let me feel her love for me as strongly as if she was sitting beside me on the couch in our living room. Don't let me doubt her in any way. More than that, give me the ability to show her how much I love her and how proud I am of the job she's doing. Amen

★ ★ ★

*Faithful love and truth will join together; righteousness and peace will embrace.*

*Psalm 85:10 HCSB*

# PROTECT OUR CONVERSATIONS
# WHILE WE'RE APART

★ ★ ★

"In conversation, humor is worth more than wit
and easiness more than knowledge."

*George Herbert*

*Dear Lord,* lately I feel like our conversations have been crowded with awkward silences. It's almost like we no longer have anything in common and don't know how to relate to one another. I find myself second-guessing everything I say when we talk. I worry about how it will come across to him.

I also analyze what he's said. I look for hidden meanings and clues that will show me he still loves me as much as in times past. I worry that he is keeping things from me about his fear or safety or well-being. Don't let the doubts creep in and crowd out our love for each other. I remember when we could effortlessly spend hours on the phone. Now even five minutes seem to drag by. What's wrong with me? How do I fix this?

Give me the tools I need to cope with my fears and doubts. Don't let me make this deployment even harder on my loved one. Show me how to share the small details that will help him understand how much I need and love him. I don't ever want him to feel like I've moved on without him. Amen

★ ★ ★

*To sum up, each one of you is to love his wife as himself, and the wife is to respect her husband.*

*Ephesians 5:33 HCSB*

# LESSON LEARNED

★ ★ ★

"Fellowship is a place of grace, where mistakes aren't rubbed in but rubbed out. Fellowship happens when mercy wins over justice."

*Rick Warren*

*Dear Lord,* let me take the lessons I've learned during my loved one's time at war and apply them to every aspect of my life. Don't let me forget the sweet times of hearing from You and knowing You answered my prayers before I even uttered them aloud. Bring to my mind the difficult lessons of continuing on, even though I wanted to give up and give in to the fear

Don't ever let me forget the faithfulness of true friends who were obedient when You urged them to pray on my soldier's behalf. Make me into a friend like that. Bring people into my life who need to hear about Your deep love and perfect peace, then help me share it with them in a way that brings them closer to You.

Give me the courage to remember the times when I was hurt and angry, and yet You didn't push me away but drew me closer until I had the peace I so desperately needed. You have been so patient and so loving with me; use me to be those things for others who are hurting. Never let me forget that You are always with me, no matter the circumstances. Amen

★ ★ ★

*And I pray that the fellowship of your faith may become effective through the knowledge of every good thing which is in you for Christ's sake.*

*Philemon 1:6 NASB*

# ABOUT THE AUTHOR

Edie Melson is a writer, blogger, teacher, and in-demand speaker, but most importantly she is a wife and mother of three sons, the eldest of whom is a Marine who served two tours in Iraq. She self-published her first book, *Fighting Fear, Winning the War at Home When Your Soldier Leaves for Battle.*

Edie is also the author of *Connections: Social Media and Networking Techniques for Writers* and has become known as one of the go-to experts on Twitter, Facebook, and social media for writers wanting to learn how to plug in. She is the co-director of Blue Ridge Mountains Christian Writers Conference, the military family blogger for Guideposts.org, social media director for *Southern Writers Magazine*, social media mentor for My Book Therapy, and senior editor for the popular writing website Novel Rocket. She's works with multiple civic and professional organizations, including Blue Star Mothers of America, the Advanced Writers and Speakers Association, and American Christian Fiction Writers. Edie and her family live in South Carolina.

Connect with her on her website, www.EdieMelson.com